DEGREES
OF
DEVIANCE

Student Accounts
of Their
Deviant Behavior

Second Edition

Edited by
STUART HENRY and ROGER EATON

Department of Sociology, Anthropology and Criminology

Eastern Michigan University

Sheffield Publishing Company

Salem, Wisconsin

For information about this book, write or call:
    Sheffield Publishing Company
    P.O. Box 359
    Salem, Wisconsin 53168
    Phone: (262) 843-2281
    Fax: (262) 843-3683
    E-mail: info@spcbooks.com

The first edition of this book was originally published by Avebury.

Copyright © 1999, 1990, 1989 by Stuart Henry

ISBN 1-879215-40-3

Printed in the United States of America

7 6 5 4 3

To the memory of Steve Box who, in a shorter life than most, inspired so many of his students with a desire to better understand the politics of deviance.

Table of Contents

Preface to the Second Edition

The original idea for this book was to describe the deviant activities of present-day students. One of the main problems when teaching sociology is that concepts are often seen as textbook issues that have little to do with real life. In many courses on deviance students are asked to read research literature so they may understand **other** people's rule-breaking behavior. But the deviant behavior that they read about has little similarity in content to the deviant behavior that they do. Published studies of deviant behavior are typically based on research conducted ten to twenty years earlier. This research is typically on people of a different age and class from the students, and is conducted by people who are as old as their parents. Because of this, conventional texts on deviance may fail to connect the deviance of others to the students' own real-life experiences.

This book bridges the gap between student experiences and the wider phenomenon of deviant behavior. It aims to prepare students for the concepts that they will subsequently encounter in deviancy textbooks. It invites students to explore how deviance is socially constructed by grounding their reading in contemporary accounts of fellow students' behavior. It is a book about student involvement in various degrees of deviant behavior, written in their own words. The accounts are based on the students' own experiences and on those of their friends and relatives. Student descriptions of rule-breaking behavior, as it is currently practiced, include married students having affairs, fraternity drinking parties, cocaine dealing, self-mutilation, nudism, vegetarianism and various explosives and weapons activities. These deviant activities take place in a variety of contexts, such as during work in bars, restaurants and stores, but also in dormitories, fraternities, gyms, and in other settings, both public and private, and both on and off campus.

Each account addresses the meaning of the deviant activity to the students. It describes the students' motives; the excuses and justifications they use to rationalize and explain their behavior; the reactions of other students, parents, and authorities; and the problems that students face when they are caught or when they have to manage the stigma of a deviant identity. These accounts were generated as part of the students' research for my course on deviant behavior. The students taking this course were trained in the methods of participant observation and interview, and were asked to submit a proposed topic of deviance that they had previously, or were currently, engaged in. The interviewees were to be restricted to three members of an intimate social network: friends, relatives or fellow workers.

The high trust between myself and the students brought some very unexpected and worrisome problems, including a planned burglary with dates, times, places, and method of entry, and a proposal from two students who wanted to steal a car in order to "get into the deviant action scene"! Both proposals, of course, were signed by the students and contained enough evidence to guarantee a criminal conviction for us all. When I pointed out that this was totally out of the question and insupportable by any criteria, and that the proposals had to be burned, the students concerned were genuinely disappointed and embarrassed at misunderstanding what participant observation meant!

The material included in this book formed one component of the students' research papers. The other components comprised: a section on methods and the moral dilemmas facing deviancy researchers; a section reviewing the literature on their chosen topic of deviance; and a comparative analysis between their study and the relevant literature. The accounts have been edited and the names of the students and places mentioned are fictitious (except in one case), so that anonymity will be preserved and inadvertent identification of those involved in the research will be minimized.

Although the original edition of the book is now ten years old, it remained very popular among professors who teach deviant behavior and students who study it. However, a lot of student papers have flowed over the grading desk since 1986, and I decided that a new edition was long overdue. I am also that much older and no longer even pretend to connect to the deviant lives of my students. As a result, my editing in this second edition has drawn on the talents of a younger keener eye, my co-editor Roger Eaton, himself recently graduated from our master's program in criminology and criminal justice, and now working in Florida's criminal justice system as a systems coordinator. Roger assessed the quality of my original selections, and we have replaced the less contemporary or less useful with selections of papers from my last ten years which he ranked with a view to current student interest. The new accounts are taken from students who took courses in deviant behavior and white-collar crime with me at Eastern Michigan University and were gathered between 1991 and 1998.

In a work such as this, the principal credit must go to the students who were prepared to share their often colorful, sometimes innovative, and occasionally sad, experiences with us all. In particular we would like to thank Eastern Michigan University graduates Laura Gach, Marc Holligsworth, Donna Robison, JoMarie Sharba and the thirteen other students whose research papers provided us with 16 additional accounts that refresh the earlier corpus of student wisdom. One of these accounts, on coping with and transcending stigma, by Staci Barker Wood, uses the author's real name by request. It came not from my course, but one taught by Mitch Berbrier, Assistant Professor of Sociology at the University of Alabama in Huntsville, from his course in Deviance and Social Control. We thank him and Staci for submitting this moving piece.

Also included in the 16 new "stories" are student accounts about eroticism such as the articles on topless dancing, student nurses as prostitutes, and eroticism on the worldwide web. Other articles focus on corruption and show how the rules of university life, whether in sport or student housing, are open to manipulation and violation. Yet others drawn from the world of student work focus particularly on deviance involved in restaurants by wait staff. Part of the reason for this is that I also teach a class on corporate and white-collar crime, which became the source for several of the new selections.

Yet another development occurred since the first edition. I became the co-author of a third edition of the text that I previously used: *The Deviancy Process*. Bud Pfuhl, the text's primary author, who is now Emeritus and living in Montana, called one day asking if I would take the torch for a new edition. We collaborated on an updated version of his work that was published in 1993. I also switched readers, and now use the excellent collection by Patricia A. Adler and Peter Adler, *Constructions of Deviance: Social Power, Context and Interaction* (1997).

As you read our new volume in conjunction with your texts, consider the central recurring themes and tie these to the enduring concepts in the sociology of deviance and through these student accounts, you will become richly informed about the deviance process. Their contribution to our knowledge shows us that student lives are much more complex than is often acknowledged and that their deviance, like all deviance, can only be adequately understood as a confluence of personal biographical experiences as these are shaped in the wider cultural-structural matrix of society. Although student deviance may develop at a university, like their general education, it only occasionally begins or ends there. When they graduate they not only have an academic degree but they will have experienced degrees of deviance, the range of which we have only just begun to explore.

Chapter 1
Introduction: Constructing Deviance

Defining Deviance and Deviants

To imagine that individual rule breakers are the villainous sole source of their deviant behavior is to credit them with too much. Worse, it is to miss much of the importance of what deviant behavior means and how it is socially constructed. Deviant behavior is a joint human enterprise. Humans construct it together, as actors and audience. They do so by making distinctions, perceiving differences, engaging in behaviors, interpreting their effects, and by passing judgments about the desirability or unacceptability of the behaviors identified.

To say that deviance is socially constructed by humans through an interactive process is to imply that: (1) there is not one reality but as many as there are groups constructing realities; (2) any appearance of a single dominating reality is no more than an abstraction and mystification of the multiple realities created in the interactive flux of everyday life; (3) there are many moralities reflecting these multiple realities; (4) there are numerous stereotypes constructed by groups as part of their means to control and contain human behaviors that are seen to deviate from and threaten their view of what counts as reality; and (5) deviance does not just happen but is created by human agents making distinctions and acting towards those distinctions as though they possessed object-like qualities.

People's standards as to what is ideal or acceptable behavior may be set in the face of real or imagined behavior that is feared or disliked. Acts

1

may be banned because of a desire to promote a particular set of values or lifestyle. Standards can be precisely specified as rules or laws, or else they may be more loosely constructed as informal norms and expectations. The laws, rules and norms take the form that they do as a result of being shaped by individual personal biographies, group pressures and processes, and by the wider societal context in which these individuals live.

Sometimes behaviors judged to be deviant are the product of precisely the same process of social construction as are the standards of those who are judging their behavior unacceptable; one groups' standards are another groups' deviance. When a government enacts food and drug legislation making the unhygienic preparation of carcass meat unlawful, it is promoting a particular set of values and making deviants out of those who prepare meat in ways deemed to be unhygienic. When a group of vegetarians declare any meat preparation and consumption "killing," they are making deviants of, among other people, the Food and Drug Administration. Both groups, however, are setting norms that are designed to promote a particular, albeit different, lifestyle.

On other occasions behaviors are constructed only because there exist norms, rules and laws banning them. It is no more the case that deviance is constructed and conducted without reference to existing standards, stereotypes and mythologies than it is that laws are constructed without reference to a perceived undesirable behavior. The two are interrelated. Deviance is co-produced by deviant actors and reactors and by its promoters and detractors. Deviance and convention are not isolated phenomena but exist in relation to each other and in relation to the wider societal and global structure in which they are set.

In order to decide whether a behavior is deviant we might resort to the familiar idea of statistical deviance. How many people do it relative to the whole population? As Emile Durkheim long ago pointed out, something is only deviant in relation to what is normal. Homosexuality is clearly deviant based on this criterion.

Alternatively, we might consider whether the behavior violates a publicly stated law or norm. Tax evasion or high school marijuana use are good examples here. Both are statistically normal but considered to be deviant on the criteria of illegality.

Or is deviance comprised of those behaviors that offend a particularly strong and vocal interest group? The expressed standards of government agencies, law enforcers, moral interest groups, local communities, sections of the media, and groups of academic commentators are involved in shaping standards against which such judgments could be made. But it is difficult to establish agreement between these different groups about what shall count as the appropriate standards since each group has its own particular ideas and interests about what is acceptable.

Further, what is deviant may be judged in terms of role expectations. What a doctor can do to another person because of his accepted role in society would get anyone else arrested for assault. The intimate sexual activities of two single people would be considered deviant if one of them was married. Here it is not the behavior itself that is deviant but the social expectations governing which social roles can be allowed to perform it.

The historical and social context also makes a difference as to whether a behavior will be judged to be deviant. Consider cigarette smoking. At certain historical periods this has been considered medicinal, a status symbol, a normal adult behavior, a nasty irritating habit and, increasingly, a crime. Where it is done also makes a difference. Smoking in the isolation of one's home is considered perfectly acceptable, provided other members of one's household have no objections to passive smoking effects. But smoking on school premises is often considered grounds for expulsion, while smoking during the production and preparation of foodstuffs may be grounds for dismissal. Recently, smoking in some public places and on domestic airline flights has been banned and even invokes prosecution and fines.

In short, deviance is constituted only in relation to that which is not deviant. It cannot be deviance without that comparison, or without those making it. This is why Durkheim and others have said crime is functional to society. Without it there is little opportunity afforded for the clarification, elaboration and maintenance of the boundaries of acceptability. In this regard deviance provides occasions for the celebration of order, and for the integration of groups and communities. But we should not neglect the flip side of this argument: that making rules, setting standards, and banning behavior is also making deviance. As Thomas Szasz has so vigorously shown, if deviance doesn't exist it would seem it must be created.

After differences in behavior have been identified and made significant, and after moralizing judgments have been drawn about their acceptability, another level of construction work is evident in the process of constituting deviance. This involves equating the person with the behavior. Here the whole person is reduced to a stigmatized status; a caricature of their total behavior is taken to represent their most important features. Unlike much of modern society, the construction of stereotypes is not a product of the industrial revolution but of something inherently human. For example, the Elizabethans were particularly adept at it. Consider the following extract from John Awdeley's *Fraternity of Vagabonds* written in 1561. Included in his "Quartern of Knaves," which lists twenty-five orders of bad servants, are the following stereotypes:

> 7. Rinse Pitcher . . . is he that will drink out his thrift at the ale or wine and be oft-times drunk. This is a licorish [greedy] knave that will swill his master's drink and bribe [steal] his meat that is kept for him . . . 16. Munch Present . . . is he that is a great gentleman, for when his master sendeth him with a present, he will take a taste thereof by the way. This is a bold knave, that sometime will eat the best and leave the worst for his master . . . 19. Dyng Thrift . . . is he that will make his master's horse eat pies and ribs of beef and will drink ale and wine. Such false knaves oft-times will sell their master's meat to their own profit . . . 24. Nunquam [never] . . . is he that when his master send him on an errand he will not come again of an hour or two where he might have done it in half an hour or less. This knave will go about his own errand or pastime.

People whose behavior is considered deviant are often involved in rejecting, deflecting, managing, or accepting this stereotyping or labelling of their identity. They do so because it is their whole person, not just the behavior, that is now morally questionable.

In considering deviant behavior, therefore, we need to examine each of the constituent aspects of the deviancy construction process. We need to explore: (1) why and how rules are made; (2) why people break rules; (3) the process that leads from their behavior being considered deviant to it coming to represent their identity; (4) how they reject, avoid, resist, manage or accept the deviant labels conferred upon them by others; and (5) how they develop new lives, either incorporating or transcending that which others would have them be.

Why People Ban Behavior

Perceived differences that are negatively evaluated are the source of much banning. The difference perceived may be in behavior. Identifying and defining a behavior draws it out from the vast array of possible behaviors as a special kind of behavior; one about which something needs to be done.

But it is not only behaviors that are seen as deviant. Ideas judged to be too extreme may also be banned. Communism and fascism are two obvious examples. Similarly appearances can be banned and stigmatized. Obvious examples are the disabled, such as the blind or crippled; the disfigured, like the Elephant Man; and those who wear outrageous clothes or hairstyles.

Although banning may be accomplished in the course of asserting a particular positive direction and intention, it is more common to think of banning as a reactive, rather than proactive, behavior done by audiences against something real or imagined. Audiences may be made up of ordinary citizens or interest groups or others organized to lobby, who Howard Becker eloquently described as "moral entrepreneurs." Such groups are no less social types than the social types their banning creates, but are simply people who feel threatened, powerless, offended or unsettled. As Steven Box has said, they become people who have the power, and sometimes the authority, to impose their judgments on others.

The process of banning and rule-making may begin with fear but quickly moves to a shared sense of danger and a belief among the fearful that the behavior in question is not going to go away by itself. Moreover, it is seen as controllable, and its control can be implemented by creating new rules, or by strengthening existing ones by extra enforcement. It is not clear why people believe that rules can directly control people's behavior, especially when much of the behavior that is reacted to is already breaking them.

Alternatively, a more symbolic motive may underlie rule-making activity, such as establishing or underpinning a particular social group's position in the society, as Joseph Gusfield has forcefully demonstrated in the case of the early twentieth century Prohibition laws.

Whether it is instrumental or symbolic, the conversion of some groups' private moralities into public issues is necessary if their concern is to gain sufficient legitimacy to warrant more formal rule-making. In this process, a principal partner is the media. They can act either as a forum for the display of concern or as an instrument for agitating it.

Clearly the range of strategies for mobilizing moral support is as wide as that available to candidates in a political campaign. Moral entrepreneurs can promote their case for a behavioral ban by associating their proposed rules with positive values or benefits to society. Particularly popular are those bans claimed to increase health or freedom. A similarly powerful impact can be achieved by associating the continued existence of questioned behavior with negative values, pointing up its threat to the mental, physical or moral fabric of organized society. Groups of moral entrepreneurs can draw respectability from the public by establishing alliances with respected members of society or by recruiting these people's testimonies, if not their person. Any endorsement by public officials takes the rule-making case towards a complete ban. Any myth-making which can be employed to exaggerate aspects of the behavior or to help hang the activity on the backs of already recognized undesirable social types will help the cause.

Ultimately, of course, the goal of banning a behavior will be met if the state can be "captured," such that laws are passed. This will empower the major law enforcement agencies to act, in the name of the whole society, on behalf of those groups with immediate concerns. At this point, the interest group can be said to have established an official ban against the behavior.

If law is not the outcome, captured institutions such as science, religion, education and public opinion are a significant creative accomplishment in the social construction of deviance. But it must not be forgotten that all of these institutions and agencies are themselves groups with interests and they may divide on the issue depending on whether these interests are advanced or threatened by the existence of a particular proposed ban. At the very least such groups are likely to graft their interests onto the proposed ban such that what emerges is some compromise position, not necessarily that which the original banners had in mind.

Not surprisingly, the chances of resisting the ban are considerably advanced if those engaged in the behavior, or those who wish to see us remain free to choose it, engage in a counter-political campaign. In this context, controversy, rather than consensus, can be claimed. In such circumstances, the law, as Austin Turk has shown us, becomes a weapon in the battle between competing interest groups and can actually create conflict by being a resource to be won.

Why People Break Rules

People have a choice about whether or not to break rules. But that choice is not completely free. It is both limited and facilitated by various structural and relational constraints. People's past experiences render some behaviors available to them as current choices, while closing off others which are not and have never been part of their behavioral scope. Their present biographical situation may encourage conventional behavior or counter it, nudging a search for more unconventional options. Put simply, people may be more or less willing to act deviantly. They are rarely coerced; but neither are they wholly free. Moreover, their choices are not equal because past experiences have been unique. But they are patterned since some social groups, such as blacks, women, the disabled, children of alcoholics, those raised in state homes, have been subject to broadly similar conditions. Yet even within these categories patterns of behavior are variable.

For most, rule-breaking is episodic, neither totally conventional, nor completely deviant. It is not just David Matza's delinquents who flirt with convention and conformity, postponing commitment and evading decision, but most of us. To do otherwise would be to submit to the tyranny of structured roles and to allow individuality and freedom to escape us. Indeed, for most, deviance is tied to particular situations and its practice is of short duration. People are often rule-breakers but rarely are they deviants if that is taken to mean that they systematically engage in repetitive and all-consuming anti-social behavior.

If people have a commitment at all, and that is questionable, it is to conventionality. They would need to transcend their culture and their interpersonal connections if it were otherwise and they would quickly become exhausted by the effort. Most people, most of the time, behave according to accepted norms. Here, as Matza has shown, commitment might best be described as partial since beliefs and values in conventionality may be temporarily suspended by virtue of the meaning that is constructed about a particular situation or event. Words and phrases may gloss over a situation in such a way that a person is freed from any moral constraint that might otherwise be felt. These morally neutralizing words may deny that one is either responsible for a potentially deviant act, perhaps claiming that "Under the circumstances I had no choice," or "I was not myself" because "I had one or two drinks." More simply they may deny that the behavior causes harm. Alternatively, they may question the right of the supposed victim to moral sanctuary on the grounds that "He asked for it," or "They had it coming," or it was "only retaliation for them hurting me." Yet another use of morally neutralizing words and phrases challenges the moral superiority of those asking condemning questions. For example, religious moral leaders like Jim Bakker and Jimmy Swaggert are cited as being self-confessedly guilty of sexual infidelity; police are pointed to as guilty of corruption and violence; senior government officials lie to Congress and sell government property to make personal profits. In a broader form, "Everybody cheats on their taxes and embezzles from their employer." To the potential deviant, the immediate group may be so important that wider and more abstract loyalties are lost to the moment as in, "I was only helping my mates." Alternatively, wider loyalties than those of secular humanity may supplant the wants of the situation. And even if all this is absent, the personal ledger of morality may still hold enough credit in its coffers to allow another expense without running a biography into the red.

Of course people may deviate because they have no particular commitment to conformity, as Travis Hirschi and his supporters have shown. If bonding relations are absent and no attachments have been formed between parents and other supposedly conventional actors, or if there is no stake in the conventional society, little involvement in its institutions, or a low level of belief in its norms and values, then deviance is likely to be very available. More accurately, we might say that convention is not particularly attractive if there is nothing in it for those in need of pleasure, and, further, nothing to lose for those who fear pain. The simple classicist model of human nature implied here accounts both for Robert Merton's innovators and Richard Cloward and Lloyd Ohlin's rationally driven delinquents, who adopt their deviant activities as an illegitimate means to conventional ends. It applies less readily to Merton's retreatists, who abandon conventional values and the means to achieve them and who slide into deviance as detachment from the apparent reality of a world to which they are unable to relate. Nor does it explain much of that which is irrational, such as the pursuit of pain and the avoidance of pleasure that characterizes some deviant behavior. Nor does it fully account for those who are highly bonded to conventional lives and institutions and yet deviate regardless, such as dentists abusing cocaine, doctors defrauding Medicare, and corporate executives embezzling from their companies. However, the rational interest model is an excellent beginning for our attempts to understand why corporations defraud the public and employ risk managers to maximize their opportunities to do so.

Clearly one of the main reasons why people may not have developed a commitment to conventional values is because they have commitment to other values. They may, as Albert Cohen has argued, have simply inverted the values of conventional society, alleviating their frustrated status position by constructing an alternative, oppositional, if rather defeatist sub-culture. Instead they might have inherited a sub-cultural commitment to alternative values either unwittingly, as a result of immersion in a culture that is outside the mainstream of American society, or as a result of being in a culture subordinate to the mainstream, or by creating a culture that is designed to replace the mainstream. Then there are those who violate rules in order to achieve certain causes and those who deviate in an attempt to advance the interests of their own deviant identities, refusing to accept the negative judgments about what they do.

To be shaped by one's background or to be shaped by the force of structural circumstance is to be in a context of past meanings from which newly created meaning is hewn. Values of convention or values of alternatives are the cloth from which new suits of deviant action are cut. Combining the meanings we have internalized from our socio-cultural environment with our personal experiences of what events and objects mean is necessary material for shaping the situation we are in at the present. But it also projects likely future courses of action; it suggests that we will have an affinity for some activities and an aversion to others. Even so, we are not forced. We can choose. The choice we make is unlikely to be something completely alien to our experience.

At most we come to the decision to commit an act of deviance with more or less openness, more or less willingness and more or less affinity or aversion. We are free to make choices in this context but we are neither certain nor compelled to act in a particular way. What tips the balance of our choice and leads us to the initial decision to take part in the deviant act may depend quite literally on how open and willing we already are. It may depend as much on how we see the act furthering our self-identity, or how it adds to what we already see ourselves as being.

Alternatively, our reluctance to commit the act may be slowly worn away by the persistent requests of those with whom we are in friendly relations. As well as providing models that can be trusted, friends may also supply sufficient justification, role performance, materials and skills to turn their next invitation to join them into our first participation. In Edwin Sutherland and Donald Cressey's terms these friends may finally tip the balance to provide our personal biographies with an excess of definitions favorable to rule violation. But it is important to recognize that it is still we who choose. The difference is that at this point in the process our circumstances, our friends, our wider socio-cultural heritage, and our personal biographical experiences have narrowed the possibilities from what was once merely one behavior in a vast array of others, to an either/or issue.

The decision to try the behavior, at least once, may come as a great release. It certainly changes the whole situation. No longer are we solely dependent on our past meanings or those communicated to us through the words and actions of participating friends. We have now created space for further decisions based on our own experience, while simultaneously making available a repeat deviant performance on a future date. If our experience of the deviant activity was bad, we may have been turned off by the behavior. Having satisfied ourselves and our persuaders that we know what it is and do not like it personally, we may be unwilling to try it again. We are susceptible to the audience's translation of the meaning of the activity from bad to neutral. But from neutral we may be prepared to try again, and once more, just to see if something was missed. Continued unfavorable experiences, or not particularly meaningful ones, are likely to leave us in conformity or even with a renewed commitment to conformity. However, the experience may be sufficiently neutral or attractive that we are more willing to try the activity if only to intensify it or simply because we have done it before and nothing particularly unpleasant happened.

After a succession of increasingly favorable experiences we may be prepared not merely to try the behavior one more time, but to actively seek it out as it increasingly becomes part of our biography. One may say that we are now turned on to the activity.

How People Become Deviants

A piece of deviant behavior does not a deviant make. Nor does the repetition of that behavior alone make a deviant. According to Edwin Lemert such activity is no more than primary deviance because it is only a part of the range of available behavior. At this stage there is no commitment and no identity transformation. The rule-breaker is simply breaking rules; no more, no less. In conversations with selves actors see their own essential being as non-deviant and the behavior is seen as incidental, or occasional. Initial participation in deviant behavior may result in repeat performances. However, to produce the more serious, and arguably less escapable, secondary deviance, it is necessary that the person publicly identified as deviant be excluded from normal activities, and that they undergo a transformation of their self-identity. Only when an actor plays out a deviant part as his/her identity, when s/he sees it as inevitable rather than selected, is a person referred to as a secondary deviant. But how does deviant activity get converted into deviant identity? This involves social reaction, moral judgment, degradation and the reconstruction of past biography.

A deviant status is one assigned to an actor by an audience on the basis of the meaning they hold of the ideas, behavior or attributes held by the actor. Essentially it is a judgment about the moral worth of a person based on the meaning of certain characteristics. The judgment is expressed in a shorthand fashion by a category, label, or stereotype. Since ideas and behaviors are chosen, deviant statuses arrived at in this way are known as achieved, whereas those relating to an actor's qualities or attributes are known as ascribed. In a sense they are both ascribed since even differences first have to be perceived in order to be later judged as significant. However, in the former case the actor is seen as being partly, if not wholly, responsible for the audience's use of labels, whereas in the latter this is not the case.

A person may achieve or be ascribed to more than one deviant status and these may be core or peripheral. A core or master status is one which takes precedence over all others that a person possesses such that the person comes to represent the thing described. A peripheral or auxiliary status, by contrast, is the expected behaviors, ideas or attributes of someone possessing a master status. As might be expected, it is usual that the moral standing of the master and auxiliary statuses are in the same direction such that both are seen as inferior.

The assignment of a deviant status does not happen overnight. To become a secondary deviant the actor needs to buy into the deviant label that the audience seeks to confer, and the audience needs to further respond to the person whose moral standing is in question.

The audience contribution to the development of a person's deviant status is to increase the formality, force, and frequency of its collective definition of the person as deviant. At the informal level audiences already have a stock of socially constructed stereotypical categories in which to place people. If no category is available, human ingenuity will exercise its creativity with flare, as was seen in the John Awdeley example mentioned earlier.

The informational content of the stereotypes is believed to be true by those using them and is usually seen as a gross distortion of the truth by those being classified. The audience works with these stereotypes, attempting to fit the suspected person into the deviant category. Anyone who engages in behavior prescribed by the category is liable for inclusion.

Once a person becomes subject to consideration for a deviant status, the audience starts to reevaluate or retrospectively review and assess all past behavior in an attempt to determine whether or not it was an instance of the stereotypical character. Only those features of a person's past biography that are consistent with the public deviant status are noted. In like manner, the audience begins to anticipate behaviors, ignoring those that are not designated by the stereotype and underscoring those that reaffirm it. At the same time the audience cuts off the actor from conventional behaviors and limits the types of activities that would confirm normality.

These processes occur once a person's ideas, behavior or attributes are seen as sufficiently different and disturbing to warrant consideration of them as deviant status. Some level of public knowledge of an actor's deviant activity is required for this to occur since a deviant status is a socially constructed identity. However, there are clearly levels of public acknowledgement of potential deviant status that result in the deviant-making process discussed above.

At the most basic level is the process of self-labelling. The way a person whose deviance is secret becomes subject to the deviant-making process is by them sharing in and observing publicly available stereotypes of deviants, and then by classifying themselves as such a person. Acting as both labeler and labelled, the person begins to restrict their own normal interaction to the company of those sharing the same attributes or behavior.

At a second level, public knowledge of the deviant activity may go beyond the group of fellow deviants to a nearby group. Beyond this the deviancy conferring process starts to become more publicly institutionalized. Labelling deviant behavior and stereotyping persons as deviant can occur in secret or in public. Secret labelling occurs in any organized setting and has been described as "the theory of office." This refers to the way workers in institutions and organizations develop a rationale in order to fulfill their work task. Members of any organization dealing with the public and serving them as customers or clients are able to classify the behavior of those with whom they deal or serve. Most service workers have shared stereotypes of those that they serve and these often involve both normal and deviant types. By classifying customers or clients, workers are able to bring order to an otherwise anonymous mass of people. However, it is very rare that these organizationally developed stereotypes are shared with the people who are being labelled. People will be treated differently by such workers but will rarely know it because the workers keep up a front. Erving Goffman's distinction between front stage and back stage is useful here since the service organization workers stereotype their customers or clients almost wholly in the back stage.

A third level in the process of conferring deviant statuses occurs publicly through institutions and organizations specifically designated for that purpose; principally law enforcement agencies, the courts, and psychiatric screening boards. In the social construction of deviants, the courts process clients with the expressed purpose of deciding whether or not they have committed a certain type of deviant activity and further, whether a public, societal level of labelling is warranted. Harold Garfinkel has described such public rituals as status degradation ceremonies, designed to significantly transform a person's identity into a lower moral status. During them, one's old identity is removed and a new one is conferred as the person undergoes a status passage. Indeed, the key issue is often not so much guilt or innocence but whether the person is the type of person capable of doing the behavior in question. The defense or advocate presents the person as favorable and normal while the prosecution or accusers present the act as one typical of the kind committed by a certain type of deviant and try to prove that the person in question has just such a biography.

Clearly the organizations and institutions that deal with deviants may also operate the theory of office. Workers in institutions charged with managing those who have been publicly designated deviant now apply their own informal and unofficial layering of deviant types in order to provide routine ways to handle this potentially more threatening group. In David Sudnow's terms these agency officials generate a range of normal to deviant deviants. At each stage of the public processing of persons suspected of deviance we have this two tier process of typing in operation: (i) labelling by agency workers, and (ii) labelling by the whole process.

A fourth level of public labelling occurs with sentencing to confinement in a place such as detention center, training school, special hospital, prison, etc., designed specifically for containing such persons. The most extreme versions of these are what Erving Goffman described as the total institution. These are places requiring the complete subordination of the person now labelled as deviant, segregating them physically and morally from non-deviants. In total institutions all aspects of the client's former identity are removed, such as personal belongings and clothing, and they are issued uniform clothing, and numbers rather than names. This mortification of the self creates a spoiled identity. Here the agency worker's own labelling and typing process is given legitimation because of the wider labelling process. As a result, the agency workers have little difficulty in revealing their labels and inflicting them upon those already publicly confirmed as a deviant. The coincidence of public and private deviant designations is the most powerful of audience statements about a person's moral identity.

Ironically, one of the only means of psychological survival that persons can employ in such a setting is to distance themselves from fellow deviants through employing their own stereotyping of fellow designated deviants. The result is that it is possible for a person, subject to such a setting, to be labelled by: (i) fellow deviants in their struggle to survive; (ii) staff in their struggle to cope; (iii) the society in their attempt to contain and control; and (iv) their outside reference groups in an attempt to avoid contamination.

Responding to Deviant Designations

A person's response to being publicly stereotyped with a deviant status can range from complete rejection to complete acceptance. Moreover, as we saw above with the case of self-labelling, it is not necessary to undergo even the first stage, let alone every stage of the process of public degradation, before a complete acceptance of the deviant identity occurs. Conversely, a person might go through the whole private and public degradation and labelling without capitulating to the label. For these reasons it is very difficult to empirically establish the contribution that audience labelling makes to the acceptance of the deviant status, as is testified by the years of debate and conflicting evidence on this issue. Thus, in considering deviant outcomes, it is necessary to suspend judgment about what caused the level of acceptance of a label and look at the various responses actors have to the labelling process.

Avoidance

Those engaging in deviant behavior do not readily acquiesce to the view that one aspect of their life determines their whole social and moral identity, especially if that identity is judged negatively to be inferior. Many designated deviants do not even entertain the thought that their activity is deviant, in spite of others' statements to the contrary. Those who avoid the labelling process do so by not even buying into the possibility that what they do is wrong or morally reprehensible. In its purest form, avoidance does not address negative evaluations. It simply ignores them. In lesser forms, actors acknowledge the existence of negative stereotypical labels but engage in a variety of dramaturgical skills and techniques in which they endeavor to renegotiate, excuse and otherwise recast the meaning of their behavior.

One of the principal avoidance techniques is diversion. This is an attempt by the actor to deflect attention from the act in question to some other issue or to put it in a broader context. This can be accomplished by the actor putting on a performance or by demonstrating a particular demeanor or attitude, such as being overly cooperative or excessively hostile. The use of personal alliances with those who are responsible for setting the formal system in operation is useful, as is a minimal social distance between the audience and the actor whose behavior is in question.

Alternatively, actors may try to draw on their bank of moral credit, asking the immediate audience to consider overlooking the questionable behavior in the light of their sum total of past behavior which, if this has been built up in advance, would lead, as Carl Klockars' metaphor of the ledger suggests, to them "coming out on the good side."

One of the classic avoidance techniques is the excuse. Excuses are statements in which the actor accepts that the activity is wrong but denies full responsibility for it. They are attempts to repair the broken social relations resulting from the activity. Excuses include denying responsibility either by blaming others, as in scapegoating, or denying being in full control at the time. Again the metaphor of the ledger can be used as an apologia and as part of an appeal to be given another chance with the implication that the behavior will not happen again.

Rejection and counteraction

Those who see others reacting to their behavior may, rather than deny responsibility, assertively reject the label and act either individually or collectively to change it. They engage in public stigma contests, conflict games, and mobilize counterprotests. They believe they are entitled to challenge that which is taken to be normal and to engage in the struggle over what counts as deviant and what should be done about it. They are the deviants who engage in politically organized activity to publicly change the views of the rest of society so that those who are influential at defining behavior will come to accept what they do.

At its simplest level individuals will employ a variety of justifications such as claiming that the act was not serious, "just a joke," or that no harm was intended, and that no harm was caused. A claim may be made that the action was taken in self-defense; that the offended had no rights to victim status because they were actually the protagonists. More assertively, the actors may deny the rights of their accusers, condemning them and others of supposedly high moral standing for similar moral digressions. They may assert that their own behavior is normal rather than deviant because "everyone is doing it." And if everyone clearly isn't doing it, they may draw out the various merits of their deviant behavior as a contribution to the betterment of humanity, such as it preventing greater harm, satisfying more moral standards, being the outcome of superior allegiances to friends or God.

Acceptance and embracement

It is not uncommon for the labelled to interpret their labels as a reward for their efforts, rather in the manner that a college student receives a degree or a Hollywood actor receives an Oscar. It is said that such deviant actors are engulfed by the role, but this denies that they actually attempt to achieve it. What is certain is that they strive to extend and expand it, developing a commitment to other activity that would further their deviant status and accepting the inevitability of their deviant career. Instead of forming groups to share the problems associated with confronting a hostile audience, these actors form groups to practice the activity and engage in further attempts to conceal it in what Jock Young has called an amplification of the original deviance. It is almost as if the social reaction to their behavior encourages further development of it.

Acceptance and self-denial

Some of those who engage in deviant behavior and are subject to the labelling process accept the audience's definition but do not feel they are able to do anything about their behavior or their situation. They feel isolated and alone and respond to their deviant identity by becoming depressed, losing any sense of self-worth and by dropping out. People responding in this way feel considerable guilt at their own bedevilment and, even though they may engage in minimal attempts to conceal their deviant identity through secrecy and information control, they are unable to escape this obsession with their own transparency as a deviant. In such a situation all the responses of others are scrutinized for any meaning indicative of rejection. Even the normal responses of others are inverted and transformed into a reflection of the actor's own negative self-image.

Acceptance and self-transformation

Yet others who feel isolated and alone accept the audience definition to the extent that they try to change themselves. This classically occurs in the self-labelling situation where, as Edward Sagarin shows, actors will form self-help groups in a collective attempt to conform to the norm. In the case of self-labelling the person is considered discreditable since the public may not yet be aware of their deviance. The discreditable, then, are heavily concerned with information management among normals or straights so that their deviant behavior maintains its secrecy. In public, the discreditable attempt to pass as normal by avoiding symbols that give away their condition. They are engaged in cuing misinformation, adopting public lifestyles that mislead or lead one to construe a different impression. Clearly devices and techniques of information management can be used by the discreditable, irrespective of whether they want to change their own identity or whether they want to continue the deviant behavior.

In the case of the discredited, the concern is very much with managing the effects of having a spoiled identity and attempting to minimize the stigma effects until such a time that the behavior or attributes have been transformed. The aim is to maintain a positive self-image. This may be achieved through de-stigmatization, in which the old stigmatized self is replaced by new, super moral action, voluntary work or altruism. The person is, in effect, building up new moral credit. It may also be achieved by transcendence in which the person achieves extraordinary success in a particular field of human endeavor. At the same time the deviant behavior or attributes are increasingly replaced by new non-deviant behavior. Here the person attempts to minimize the old deviancy by pointing out that they are changing, that they have many more dimensions to their life than that indicated by their past deviance, and that everyone has potentially stigmatizing problems.

Becoming Normal

In order for anyone designated with the stigma of a deviant label to become normal, they have to ultimately recognize what normal is. As I stated at the outset, normality is not the complete absence of deviance. It is, rather, the presence of deviance as one of a range of behavioral options. Occasionally, normal identities are free to choose deviance without serious moral implications for self or others. Its choice does not bring about any questioning of the actor's identity, nor does it raise the specter of some real deviant identity lurking beneath the surface should the behavior be exposed. Being normal is being free to choose deviance without serious consequences and not choosing it most of the time. But how can someone who has suffered serious challenge to their identity resume their former position of normality? Clearly, forming relations of mutual support with fellow deviants does not return an actor to normalcy because most of those who have not been stigmatized do not have relations with others based solely on their participation in a morally condemned behavior. While self-help groups are a transition to normality, they are not its final resting place. This lies in the ability of those stigmatized to select, from all those with whom they formerly had relations, only those who maintain an open-minded, supportive relationship. It also requires that new relations be formed such that interaction of the present begins to construct a new biography which eventually builds to form its own history. All of this may require a change of location; it certainly requires sufficient confidence to award oneself the right to be normal. In short, it requires that the deviant who seriously does not want to be so cast, cease to invest in that which gives pain and to start again, building a new life and a new identity.

Studying Deviance

Studying deviance, then, is about studying how human agents interact with each other and how, in doing so, they create differences, act them out, pass judgments and act on those judgments in relation to each other. Fundamentally, it is the study of how people classify each other, about how those classifications are morally evaluated as good and bad, and about the devices and the power through which they exert their view of what is to be taken as real. It is, at the same time, a study of the fear of innovation, difference and change; an inquiry into a human struggle to transcend the limits of convention and familiarity that people allow to be imposed on themselves and on their own creative energies through a process of social stereotyping.

Clearly the methods one uses to capture the meaning of deviance must be sufficiently sensitive to appreciate the fine twists and turns, the hidden motives and agendas that are the hallmark of those who are involved in its daily construction. The principal method that has characterized the social constructionist approach to deviance is the ethnography or, in its sociological form, participant observation. Put simply, this demands that the student of deviance get sufficiently involved in the action to be able to understand the members' meanings and yet remain sufficiently neutral so that the research can proceed with a degree of objectivity. This is best achieved by the student having a dual role; hence participant-observer. The articles which comprise this book have been based on just such a methodology, supplemented by interviews with the participants. In each case the student authors were not only members of the deviant action scene, but were also students of deviance.

Themes in the Readings

As you read this book it will become apparent that there are certain key themes held in common by a diversity of deviant actors. Patterns of deviance can be identified from accounts about their deviant behavior. The central themes that come out of this exploration of student deviance are the following.

1. The difference between types of deviant behavior may be less significant than the similarities in their motives and rationalizations. Deviant typologies, like criminal typologies, are social constructions that enable us to make sense of the actions of those who break rules; they are not necessarily real and we may learn more by suspending our expected acceptance of such common sense definitions of reality.

2. Many different kinds of deviance have similar motives and these motives are often no different from the motives for conforming behavior. The following classification is neither exhaustive nor mutually exclusive but includes many of the motives most commonly constructed by participants of deviant activity and which can be found in the accounts in this book:

(a) **Pecuniary, material or tangible motives:** to make money, to obtain goods or services, to obtain sex

(b) **Recreational motives:** to enjoy fun and excitement; to obtain thrills, to play; to get high; to beat the system (seen as a game)

(c) **Interpersonal or social motives:** to achieve status; to earn honor and prestige; to repay favors; to gain acceptance, fit in or feel normal; to stand out; to express friendship, loyalty or resentment; to fulfill role expectations; to compete or meet a challenge

(d) **Problem-solving motives:** to relieve pain, stress, tension or boredom; to establish identity; to compensate for missing expectations; to cope; to avoid or escape responsibility; to preserve self (self-defense); to restore control over one's life

(e) **Political motives:** to correct injustices; to gain domination over others; to gain freedom from others; to beat an oppressive system; to change society or parts of the social system; to express allegiance to alternative religious, moral or ethical beliefs

It might be more appropriate, therefore, to classify deviance by its motives rather than by the behavioral category by which we identify it. What should be clear, however, is that the motives for deviance are the same as the motives for conventional behavior. Thus, explaining deviance by the use of motives is no more instructive than saying people deviate because of the particular culture they share. In either case what remains unexplained is why some people with similar motives or culture deviate while others do not.

3. As part of their social construction of motive, the following range of neutralization techniques is employed by deviants or is found as part of the social context that can release them from the consequences of considering the opinions of those who condemn their actions:

(a) Denial of responsibility (e.g. "It's not my fault.")

(b) Denial of injury (e.g. "No one gets hurt.")

(c) Denial of victim (e.g. "They have hurt me and do not deserve consideration.")

(d) Condemnation of condemners (e.g. "The judges are criminals.")

(e) Appeal to higher loyalties (e.g. "My friends are more important than society's laws.")

(f) Metaphor of the ledger (e.g. "In the final analysis I come out on the good side.")

(g) Claim of normality (e.g. "Everybody does it.")
(h) Denial of intent (e.g. "It was just a joke.")
(i) Claim of relative acceptability (e.g. "There are worse people than me.")
(j) Claim of individuality (e.g. "I don't care what anyone else thinks.")

It should also be apparent that these techniques of neutralization may be employed after the deviant activity to rationalize behavior, maintain a sense of moral purity, normalize a biography, or relieve one of the culpability for any consequences of the act. They may also be employed after the act has been contemplated but before it has been committed, thereby acting as a motive. (e.g. If sufficient social acceptance of the rationalization is attributed to the excuse or justification, a person may feel relatively free to engage in the activity.) Finally, they may be used by others in the course of non-deviant behavior, so reducing a person's commitment to morality and rendering them free, but not compelled, to commit the deviant activity.

4. Legal, social, or moral sanctions that exist on a society-wide basis are not particularly effective against those people who are members of sub-cultural groups.

5. The most effective controls, or at least the ones that those who deviate seem to express most concern over, are those emanating from people from whom they have low social distance, such as relatives, friends, and members of the same deviant subculture. Those people who have high social distance from rule breakers are least effective at controlling behavior of those who deviate.

6. Stereotyping has been shown to be employed to create deviants as well as control deviants.

As we have seen, a recurring theme in these accounts is striving to show that we are different, that each of us is someone to take notice of, that we are in some important senses capable of shaping the world in which we live. But we also see that even when we strive to be different our interaction with others binds us to conform. That we don't conform to wider societal morality and law is no evidence that we don't conform, for our very joining with others who share our deviant activity is an indication of the force of those around us. We declare independence when we say that we don't care what others think but we reveal our vulnerability in our sensitivity to what friends and co-deviants think. We are individuals but we are also social beings. We might be able to tilt the balance, but it is the extreme deviant who is unaffected by aspects of both these internal and external forces.

What we learn from this study of student accounts of their deviance will depend in part on our own values and interests. It will also depend on how far we are able to suspend our moral judgments in order to appreciate why they are doing things we find offensive and objectionable. Without suspending such judgments it would have not been possible to obtain the trust of those students who contributed often incriminating, sometimes self-deprecating, accounts to this volume and we would not have been able to know how they constructed these aspects of their lives. For that we would be informationally poorer.

We reject the view of those who say that explorations of diversity render us culturally and morally rudderless; that giving every meaning credibility, every identification of difference, legitimacy, means that we can ultimately say nothing. Deviance is both a celebration and condemnation of diversity. Diversity enables us to adapt to changing circumstances. It gives us the possibilities to survive. Conformity is tied to what is. To recognize diversity is saying a lot. It is saying that we are not completely bound by the constraints of past structures or current constructions of reality, that our own agency can make a difference, that what you think matters. That the difference made is one that some, or even many, find offensive should not blind us to the importance of the struggle. We all have to make a difference. It should alert us to the fundamental importance of societal institutions and broader structures to facilitate the means of individual recognition, for it will emerge if we try to suppress it and its emergence may not please us. Does this exploration of deviance mean that we cannot make moral judgments? Of course it doesn't. We can make much more informed judgments than those we would have made without the appreciation and understanding of those who take part in deviant behavior. To understand the meaning of a deviant activity and then to weigh that activity in the light of a wider social context is to make a responsible judgment about the activity. To fail to attempt to understand that to which we object is taking the same irresponsible attitude that we find offensive in others. We do not care. Why should they?

We began this book by suggesting that its main aim was to draw on student accounts of their deviant behavior in order to provide a bridge to central concepts in the sociological literature on deviance. In itemizing the central themes that emerge from these many micro studies we hope that the final stages of the bridge's structure have been laid. Ultimately, however, a bridge is not a bridge until it is walked over, and only you can do that. In the final analysis you have to make the connections between the sociological literature that you read and the materials that these students have presented here.

Recommended Reading

Adler, Patricia A. and Peter Adler. *Constructions of Deviance: Social Power, Context and Interaction*. Belmont: Wadsworth, 1997.

Becker, Howard S. *Outsiders: Studies in the Sociology of Deviance*. New York: The Free Press, 1963.

Box, Steven. *Deviance, Reality and Society*, 2nd Edition. New York: Holt, Rinehart and Winston, 1981.

Deutschmann, Linda B. *Deviance and Social Control*, 2nd Edition. Scarborough, ON: ITP Nelson, 1998.

Goffman, Erving. *Stigma: Notes on the Management of Spoiled Identity*. Englewood Cliffs, NJ: Prentice Hall, 1963.

Goode, Erich. *Deviant Behavior*, 5th Edition. Upper Saddle River, NJ: Prentice Hall, 1997.

Henry, Stuart. *The Hidden Economy: The Context and Control of Borderline Crime*. Oxford: Martin Robertson, 1978; republished by Loompanics Unlimited, Port Townsend, WA, 1988.

Herman, Nancy J. *Deviance: A Symbolic Interactionist Approach*. Dix Hills, NY: General Hall, 1995.

Kelly, Delos H. *Deviant Behavior: A Text-Reader in the Sociology of Deviance*, 5th Edition. New York: St. Martin's Press, 1996.

Little, Craig B. *Deviance and Control: Theory, Research and Social Policy*, 3rd Edition. Itasca, IL: F. E. Peacock, 1995.

Matza, David. *Delinquency and Drift*. New York: John Wiley and Sons, 1964.

_____. *Becoming Deviant*. Englewood Cliffs, NJ: Prentice Hall, 1969.

McCaghy, Charles H., James K. Skipper, Jr., and Mark Lefton. *In Their Own Behalf: Voices from the Margin*, 2nd Edition. Englewood Cliffs, NJ: Prentice Hall, 1974.

Pfohl, Stephen. *Images of Deviance and Social Control: A Sociological History*, 2nd Edition. New York: McGraw-Hill, 1994.

Pfuhl, Jr., Erdwin H. and Stuart Henry. *The Deviance Process*, 3rd Edition. New York: Aldine de Gruyter, 1993.

Schur, Edwin M. *The Politics of Deviance: Stigma Contests and the Uses of Power*. Englewood Cliffs, NJ: Prentice Hall, 1980.

Chapter 2
Erotic Activities

In the first article by Janet we learn about cheating in relationships. Janet shows how involvement in deviance can develop slowly as potential deviants repeatedly frequent the same social setting. Here the affair emerges from a conventional situation, and it only becomes deviant because the participants are married. In the same context, anyone else who was behaving similarly would be acting conventionally. This demonstrates the importance of personal biography, social roles and their interrelated normative expectations in the social construction of deviance. Janet's article highlights the importance of friends as facilitators in bringing about eventual involvement in the activity.

The second article by Jill takes place in the "Stripmall," a high-class topless dancing establishment, which boasts the "most beautiful women in the state." Here the dancers, including author Jill, are themselves students. Some also are single moms and their deviance involves various forms of deviant extra services and "dating" of businessmen, provided they have demonstrated their willingness to pay. These services are informally arranged and deviate from the club rules which forbid the activity. Through her interviews with fellow student strippers, Jill identifies the motives of power, control, and money that the dancers say free them from control by others, and reveals the mutual support among strippers, as well as the way they control coworkers' deviance. Especially informative is the way in which these women feel justified that what they are doing is necessary, temporary, and even, in some cases, a service to their customers.

In contrast, the third article deals with the erotic activity of lap dancing, prostitution, and drug taking that takes place in a low-class strip bar. Karen tells us the story of an average night, in which drugs, illegal sex, and tip stealing occur at the Golden Bow. Lap dancing generates the money to fund the women's drinking and drug taking in a cycle that enables the dancers to get up on stage and to deal with all sorts of different types of men for whom most of the workers have contempt.

In the last account Tyrone introduces us to the often superficial world of virtual sex through Internet chat lines. He demonstrates that in spite of attempts to control the activity it is extensive and offers access to sex talk and pornography without the consumer leaving the safety of their home or office. Tyrone shows us that anyone can gain easy access and that they can also change identities, freeing themselves from stigmatized roles or bad reputations. Finally, he explains how for some members of these chat lines the net has removed restrictions to what they see as a more liberated society, free from the rules and the consequences of violating society's restrictions.

A range of motives is revealed in these contributions. All of these cases show the importance of fun and excitement in doing something that is considered deviant. But we learn, also, how the opportunity to deviate becomes more attractive when the actor's ideals and expectations regarding conventional roles and socially structured opportunities are not being satisfied. Janet tells how the expectations of a conventional marriage, such as emotional support, trust, respect, and honesty, may fail to be met by one's spouse. In such a situation a person may become ready and willing to deviate in order to compensate for the failure of conventional roles. Janet gives examples of how the compensation motive may be particularly strong when, for some structural reason such as a missing spouse, conventional satisfactions are absent. Here the unconventional will act as a substitute, relieving the tension of being temporarily denied what one has come to expect.

We should not neglect those who cheat in relationships in order to conform to their own image of themselves. This desire might have resulted from one's self-image having been tainted or undermined through conventional relationships. Alternatively, it might have become routine for the individual to episodically demonstrate their social status, in this case manhood or womanhood, through acts which, by other criteria, are judged deviant. Ego satisfaction is the simplest description of this motive, although, as such it can range from reasserting ego through indulging or creating it.

The motives for the student strippers in Jill's story are not as complicated. Traditional jobs, such as a waitress or retail salesclerk, do not pay all of the bills. College students' incomes are very low, college fees are high and good jobs are hard to find, especially when you can only work part-time because of schoolwork. Therefore, using their bodies for sex generates extra cash for paying off debts. As Jill illustrates, the money she can earn from "dancing" and the extra dollars that come from serving needy men, help not only pay for college but also go to support these single parents' children. And, as she points out, strippers are in control of their own destiny in ways that student grants, loans, and parents cannot begin to match.

Rationalizations, justifications and excuses are the words used to make sense of why we act the way we do. But they are intertwined with motives, since if we can find the reason why we might justify or excuse a particular behavior, we might find this is sufficient reason to engage in it; the words themselves become the motive. As Janet's friends illustrate, it is reassuring to describe deviance as compensation for what we should justifiably have, since then we can believe that we are simply satisfying universal emotional needs under difficult circumstances. And for Jill, the men who want to date her, albeit against the house rules, are not always interested in sex. They may just want the company of an attractive, female companion, which lends itself to the justification that both the dancer and their date are gaining from the relationship. As one of her coworkers explains, "We actually helped that guy and his marriage. There are worse things we could do for money,"—observations which mesh well with ideas about "appealing to higher loyalties" (than the law, morality or the rules) and claiming relative acceptability. This is also reflected in the comments of one of Tyrone's sex chat line interviewees who claimed that she "was only exercising her true right as a woman to exceed the sexual limitations placed on her by a closed-minded society."

A number of other ways of retaining a morally pure sense of self are introduced in these five studies. The classic denial of injury or harm is actually used by some of Janet's friends to continue to conceal their activity, on the basis that the problem is not in the doing but in those who would be hurt knowing about it. Denial of injury is also used to justify dating customers by Jill's dancers who believe not only that no one is getting hurt, but that, in fact, their customers are being helped. Indeed, we possibly see the "metaphor of the ledger" at work in the veterinary student and coworker of Jill, whose stripping is offset by her charity work for fire victims, adopt a child, gift giving and animal rights concerns.

Another technique for making the erotic activity morally acceptable is to distinguish it from something more reprehensible and, in effect, to redefine the boundary of what is acceptable and what is not. For example, Karen believes that taking drugs while dancing is a part of the job and that this is better than drug addicts who are jobless and live on the streets. Another example is that some of Janet's friends will distinguish between what they take to be real cheating in relations, which involves having sexual intercourse outside a marriage, and being "just friends," which they define as acceptable. An additional device used here is to stick to the letter, rather than the spirit, of the rules, as in "I am not breaking any of the agreements that I've made."

Finally, these articles indicate that the right of those who morally condemn others can be questioned. Since those taking part desire that their own situation and feelings be considered, then failure to do this puts the condemners at moral fault. It is the condemners who don't understand, which in turn negates the import of their indignation. Such condemning also encourages, and justifies, secrecy designed to protect self as well as reducing the likelihood of being caught. Excuses, justifications, and the secrecy with which the activity is conducted go a long way in enabling those who participate in erotic activities to avoid having to deal with any stigma that might otherwise be conferred upon them.

Affairs
by Janet Frost

We were all married students who had or were having affairs. Each of us got involved by going out to nightclubs without our spouses. We never intended to get involved with anyone, initially. It was just a night on the town with the guys or girls. After going out alone, you start to meet interesting people. Eventually we got involved with someone. Larry describes how he met one of his ex-girlfriends: "I met her through a friend at a club. She was talking to a friend of mine. I had seen them together and noticed he wasn't treating her right. So I told her to leave him alone because he wasn't any good. The next night I asked her out."

Larry and Andrea found it easy to cheat on their spouses because their marriages were not supplying them with all of their needs. Larry's marriage lacked emotional support. He said his wife was a constant nag. His relationships with other women provide him with "peace of mind, happiness and comfort in knowing that he could enjoy life with someone." Similarly, Andrea was not getting the respect and trust she wanted and expected from her husband: "I love my husband and he's a good person but he has a lot of bad ways about him." Andrea explained, "I just want someone I can really open up to." She gets this and more from her friend: "There are a great many rewards and the main ones are trust and honesty.

It's satisfying just to have someone enjoy you as a person from within his heart; someone who thinks of you as intelligent and not just having a nice figure or pretty face; someone who doesn't just want to go to bed with you."

Unlike Larry and Andrea, Brenda saw her relationship with her spouse as a loving and caring one. Her reason for having affairs was quite simply that her husband was not always home. She is a full-time college student and her husband is in the navy and spends a lot of time away at sea. She dates other people "just for the fun of it," and to get out of the apartment. She flirts with guys a lot and enjoys it: "I find it very exciting to flirt. It is very flattering to know that other men are interested in me. It makes me feel good about myself that someone besides my husband finds me attractive."

Larry also found that affairs served an important function in promoting his self-image. He saw his behavior as a game and as a way to prove his manhood to himself. As he reflected, "After being with one person for a long period of time you sometimes feel that you have to prove something to yourself, to prove that you've still got what it takes to be a man. You can do this by getting someone of the opposite sex to be attracted to you and to see how far you can get them to go."

Whether or not these affairs were seen as cheating seemed to depend upon whether sex was involved. Brenda did not see her relationships as cheating: "I'm not sleeping with these people. Females as well as males can have friends of the opposite sex without any type of sexual involvement." Similarly Andrea said, "Who says you can't have a friend? I haven't broken any of my vows and I don't plan on it. I'm not sleeping with my friend and we don't have sex or do anything sexually. Having a friend is not cheating. Having a friend and sleeping with him is cheating."

In spite of the fact that they personally saw nothing wrong with their behavior, neither Brenda nor Andrea are prepared to tell their husbands about their relationships with other men. Andrea said that she cared about her husband's feelings and didn't want to hurt him. She also said that she believed in the saying, "What you don't know won't hurt you." Brenda said that she would never tell her husband because he is the jealous type. She is afraid how he would react to the fact that she has male friends and "might go crazy and destroy everything in his way."

All agreed that their family, friends and others would probably view their behavior as cheating. They were aware that the distinction they made between having a friend of the opposite sex and being sexually involved with someone besides their husbands would not be accepted by others. This was more a reason for not telling than it was for refraining from the activity. Brenda said, in a soft low voice, "My family would feel really bad about me cheating on my husband. I don't want them to know. It would hurt them too much."

Andrea and Larry did not care what other people thought of their relationships. Larry said, "I don't care what the rest of society thinks. I'm doing what I want and what makes me happy and that is all I care about." Andrea used the same kind of justification. She said that she did not see why she should be miserable for other people: "They are living their lives and I have to live mine. If they hate the idea of me seeing someone and being married then they are not considering my feelings and whether or not I am happy. I am happy with my friend and with our relationship. I'm making my own decision about my life. I find it objectionable for other people to tell me what to do with my life."

"Dating" for Money
by Jill Turner

The "Stripmall" is considered to be one of this state's premier gentlemen's clubs. Along with excellent sound and lighting systems and top-rated businessmen's lunches, they boast the state's most beautiful topless women. There are many rules governing the dancer's interaction with customers which are designed in part to reduce the chances of violating the licensing laws and partly to maintain the club's respectability. As Tom Napoleon, the owner of the club said, "We are not a dating service. Our girls are professional entertainers, not prostitutes. By setting this standard we have effectively kept the quality of our dancers higher than any club in the state and have kept out the bad element." The rules are strict and violations can result in punishments varying from $25 to $100 in fines, and include suspensions, denial of scheduling requests and, ultimately, termination. In addition the dancers themselves develop their own rules about what is and is not acceptable and their own ways of regulating this activity, such as ostracization and harassment by coworkers, including stealing their costumes, makeup and money.

While the whole issue of professional entertainers, that is topless dancing, could be considered deviant, within this context there are other deviant behaviors that violate both the house rules and the dancers' own rules. One of the club rules is NO CONTACT and another is that NO DANCER SHALL DATE A CUSTOMER FOR FINANCIAL GAIN. By and large most of the dancers abide by the no dating rule, but stories abound about who is seeing who after work and for how much. The stereotypical reputation that dancers have as whores is a result of this rule violation.

The "Stripmall" operates three stages, so three different women are on stage at all times. The club operates on two shifts and averages 25 girls per shift. Each dancer takes her turn on stage and then is free to circle the floor in search of customers who would like a table dance ($10) or a couch dance ($20). Dancers approach customers and after some conversation and maybe a drink the customer is offered a dance. A couch dance is performed upstairs in a semi-private setting and the dancer gets as close and personal as possible without breaking the club's no contact policy. It is here, against club policy, that the opportunity for an exchange of phone numbers and date planning is most frequent.

On a typical day a few of the girls arrive two hours early for work. We sit in the dressing room, drink coffee and talk about our lives. The discussion often involves activities that are not discussed with those outside this group, an atmosphere that promotes closeness and honesty among our group of strippers. I talked with three strippers ranging in age from 22-26, each of whom has been in the business for over 2 years and considers this work her main source of income.

Candy is a 26-year-old stripper who has been in this business for over 9 years. She began as a coat check girl and progressed to waitress and finally to a stripper 5 years ago. Candy and I went to dinner with regular customers several times over the past month. For each dinner date we were paid $500. Candy reported to me that going to dinner with customers occasionally will keep them interested in her and let them maintain their belief that she actually likes being with them. It also keeps them coming back to the club to see her where they spend more money on her.

Candy also gets positive recognition from management at the club as a result of her rule-breaking behavior. "I know it is against the rules, but Tom (club owner) compliments me on the fact that I have so many return customers coming in asking for me. He appreciates my loyalty to his club and ignores the fact that I am breaking rules because in the long run he is making more money too. Hell, last year he gave me a gold necklace for Christmas. You have to be pretty good to get that out of him."

Candy is not only motivated by economic gains but also by social rewards. She says, "I go to the best restaurants in town. I am seen in the nicest clothes and always ride in the finest cars. I like that and feel important. Whenever there is a high profile event in town you can bet I am there in style." As a result of this "side work," Candy has been subject to stigma but has resisted the personal impact that it might have by surrounding herself with others who do not condemn what she does. She laughs at these other girls who she says are stupid: "This is a dog eat dog world. I know what it takes to make it. Obviously they are not smart enough to compete with me. As long as I like who I am, what does it matter what those poor girls think?"

Another one of the girls, Morgan, also uses the club as a meeting place for her customers. She sets up all of her dates from the club; some of them involve sex and others don't. Morgan will not date a customer who has not come to see her at least four times, and they must spend some money on her each time. She views her time at the club as a screening process. In an effort to maintain her secret deviant status, she will only exchange sex for money with customers who are married: "If a guy is married, it cuts down on the bullshit. He won't make demands on my time or run his mouth. He has more to lose than I do. My customers all understand that I am a mother and a student. I plan to leave this place and them as soon as I graduate. Their money allows me to be both a good student and a mom. As soon as I can support my family on a normal job's pay, I am so outta this crazy life." She claims that the label "tramp" that others see her as "will not always be her." As a recent divorcee and single parent, now having her own money, she feels free from her ex-husband's demands or threats of holding back child support. This freedom and control provided by stripping echoes the findings of others, who see both stripping and dating customers as providing a power and control for women who feel out of control or who are controlled by others.

Tiffany, a 25-year-old veterinary student, is in her final year and is in the top of her class. Tiffany makes it well known to anyone who will listen that she is retiring from the business a week after graduation. She takes great pride in having made it through school without her parent's help, or the government's aid program. Tiffany is known by her coworkers as "Charity." She collects money for local victims of fires and also leads the club's adopt-a-family at Christmas program. Her locker is adorned with human and animal rights articles. She is the one who organizes birthday gifts for coworkers as well as regular customers.

Tiffany drives to the club two days a week from her home which is over one hundred miles away. She has worked very hard to maintain her status as a secret deviant: "I drive so far to work so the chances I'll see anyone who knows me from real life are slim. No one knows my real name and I only date customers who are aware of my need for secrecy and are in the same boat. " She says, "As long as I am in this business I cannot have a serious relationship. What kind of a man would want someone who does what I have to do for money?"

I attended a date with Tiffany from its conception to the conclusion. This particular date is known as a regular in the club. He was getting a dance from Tiffany and began to complain that his wife is going through menopause and that he really needed to talk to someone about it before he went crazy. So Tiffany arranged for the three of us to have dinner after work. While we discussed the effects of menopause, Steve's spirits seemed to lift. After dinner Steve gave us some money and thanked us repeatedly. As soon as Steve left, Tiffany commented, "Don't you feel good? We actually helped that guy and his marriage. There are worse things we could do for money." Tiffany admits though that not all of her dates are of the talking kind. She has convinced herself that the service she provides helps other people, doesn't hurt anyone and gives her economic stability.

These girls agreed that they are aware that people's misunderstanding of their business or fear of them is understandable because people only see the bad side. On one occasion we discussed Demi Moore's movie "Striptease." Morgan commented: "That woman spent two weeks in a strip club and she's a millionaire. How could she possibly make a movie that was anywhere near realistic? When will someone make a movie that shows the real us—the struggles, the fears, the responsibility and the physical effort it takes to do this? No wonder everyone looks down on us with crap like that out there."

In the past year the laws and county ordinances have put additional pressures on both the club owners and the strippers. As a result of negative press clips and the sensationalization of the extreme cases concerning the activities on the "8 mile strip" (an area with seven strip clubs in a three-mile radius), local politicians found it necessary, and even advantageous, to address what it called a public outcry demanding attention to the illegal prostitution. These activist politicians whipped up support and forced local agencies to begin a vice operation to fine club owners and ticket individual strippers for lewd behavior and soliciting prostitution. Two clubs were forced to shut down as a result of law violations. The raids were highly visible in the news. Strippers and customers were paraded in front of local news cameras in handcuffs. This resulted in declined business for the remaining clubs and a higher concentration of strippers in the clubs. Candy commented, "Because there are so many girls here I have to go further to make the same amount of money as I did last year." And going further means dating our customers for extra money.

Sex, Drugs and Dancing Girls
by Karen Shaw

It's Friday night at the Golden Bow. The night crew has to be there at 6:45 PM. At 7:00 PM there's a shift change. At this time, the day crew is in the bathroom selling drugs to the night crew. The favorite drug at the bar is "coke." The dayshift is drunk and high. This is easy to see.

At the beginning of the night not much is going on. Before the bar gets busy, the dancers hang out in the bathroom. Most of the time, when they are in there, a lot is going on. The girls who do drugs "hang" together. Laura doesn't really "hang" with anyone because of the drugs she does. Her high involves needles. She also smokes crack, coke, and pot and tops it off by drinking Southern Comfort. This kind of a mixed high is not unusual for this bar. On this particular Friday night the same girls are doing the same drug thing.

Drug use is not limited to the dancers. Some of the waitresses do them too. The difference is that the dancers have more time in the bathroom—so they can do more drugs. Tonight I see Carrie (a waitress) sitting in the corner of the bar, alone. She has her head down on the table, as if she is resting. There is only a handful of people in the bar at the time, so no one cares if she rests. After a second look I see she's really doing lines of coke off the table.

Selling drugs in this bar is easy. You can easily recognize the players. They are the ones all the girls talk to. After talking they go to the bathroom for a short time. Tonight a dancer and a waitress are both selling in the bar. This doesn't work out too well. The two girls end up in a fight over whose night it is to sell. The blood is hot and it's not yet even 8:00 PM.

Most of the dancers and waitresses have a drinking problem, at least while they are at work. There are two basic reasons why they get high on drink or drugs. One is to get the courage to get up on stage and the other is to deal with the kind of people we get in here.

The drinking continues all through the night. Lorraine started out the night with a shot and a beer. She does this regularly. She is a dancer so she can do it and no one can tell she's drunk until it is too late. The backs of her legs and her back are covered with marks. This is from where her misjudgment has caused her to fall off the stage or tables. Lorraine always gets back up on the stage. I don't believe she feels anything at the time—she's too drunk. I'm sure she'll feel it in the morning. I'm also sure she'll fall off the stage again tonight.

About the time the bar starts to get busy, the waitresses and dancers are feeling "good" and ready to go to work. The other dancers begin showing up. These are the ones only working for the tips they get while dancing.

The dancers that were here at the start of the night have already found some customer to sit with them, who will buy them a drink and who will tip them too.

It is at this time some of the sex acts take place. You can tell which customers are the ones who would try anything. They sit in the dark corners or the booths. These guys figure they can do anything they want if they buy a girl a drink or give her a few dollars.

The sex acts occur between customers and dancers and waitresses alike. They can range from putting dollar bills down the girl's shirt or G-string (to get a quick feel), to sitting there with the girl when he has his hand between the upper part of her legs.

On this Friday night our usual men are there. They always sit in the same booths and shortly afterwards someone, Gloria, sits down with them. Quickly afterwards she gets "the busy hands." Gloria doesn't seem to mind as she quickly consumes her drink and orders another. Mr. "Busy Hands" pays happily.

"Lap dances" are another way of providing sex acts for money. In a lap dance, the dancer literally dances in your lap, often fondling and rubbing you with both her hands and body. There are no limits. Chrissy is dancing and doing lap dances—at least we think so. But it's really sex: the guy paid her one hundred dollars to have sex with him. Chrissy gets on the guy's lap and starts to grind. This turns him on. He tips her more money for more action. She removes part of the guy's pants and she pulls aside her G-string. This way when you look at her you can't really tell what is going on unless you take a second look.

Kelly, a waitress, was accused of stealing twenty dollars from a customer. This is a common way of making more tips from the ones who don't tip. These thefts generally happen later in the night when the customers are too drunk to notice. I believe that on this occasion Kelly took the money. She does a lot of drugs (crack) and she was out all night last night. Last night when she left the bar she had made some good tips. When she came to work tonight, she was broke. There have been times in the past when Kelly has sold drugs for a man. Her part of the profit is free drugs.

At about midnight, one of the waitresses is missing. No one knows what has happened to Tina. She's taken off during the night in the past and not told anyone. We figured this was a repeat performance. About this time the place gets a little crazy.

The dancers are high and drunk. Several of the waitresses are too. There are two dancers on stage together. They are dancing for each other. They appear to be almost ready to have sex with each other right there on the stage. The customers are loving it and are tipping the two on stage very well. The manager is at the end of the bar. She's judging a contest for the "Biggest 'Cock' of the Night."

Vanessa, a dancer, is doing a lap dance. Afterwards the man does not want to pay her. She gets mad, takes off her high-heel shoe and hits him between the eyes! Then she grabs the money and runs to the bathroom.

Next to our bar is a gay bar. On Friday nights the gay bar has a form of a beauty contest where the men show up dressed in drag. This night three men who are dressed like women come in to our bar to be picked up by some men who don't know they are really men. The DJ spots the three men as they come in. As a joke he sends a drink to one of the three men/women. The waitress is in on the joke and tells one that the drink is from one of the men at the bar. This guy is a regular. The man/woman comes over to the bar to thank the guy who sent the drink over to "her." The guy at the bar had no clue what was going on.

At 1:30 in the morning, the local drug dealer comes in to make his last sale of the night and to pick up some money from one of the dancers. As soon as he walks in the door, most of the dancers and a few of the waitresses go up to him. He stays for a few drinks and takes off.

Closing time finally comes. There are plenty of drunk people in the bar (customers and employees alike). In the back of the bar in a booth is our missing waitress. She had drunk too much, gone back there and passed out. A few customers are waiting for some of the girls—they were giving them a ride home. Every night there are different men waiting.

I think I am the last employee to leave, when all of a sudden I hear a groaning noise in the bathroom. It sounds like someone is getting hurt. The bathroom door is locked from the inside. I start to go get the keys for the door, when the door opens and out come the two dancers that were dancing for each other earlier, and the DJ whose zipper is down.

This is a typical night. It ended about the same way it does every night—Lorraine fell off the stage.

When anyone asks the day manager about drug use and drug sales going on at the Golden Bow during his shift, his reply is, "Oh no, not my girls! You must be thinking of the night shift." He wants to conceal it from others and himself. No one's fooled.

Sue is one of the dancers. She said, "Just look around. It's there. You just have to look and see it." I asked Sue to explain some of the activities that happen. "That's easy," she informed me. "Drug use is common because it helps a person deal with the customers. The sale of drugs is hard for a dancer to do. I tried it for awhile, but it wasn't worth it to me. The risk is too high."

When asked if there are any pressures from the other dancers to get involved in drug use and sex she said, "Yes, if you don't join in and do what the others do, they keep pushing until you feel weird." I asked her what she would not do. "Slutting is what I'm talking about. The guys are not called 'tricks' they are called 'friends.' You don't hook for money, but rather you 'go out with a friend and make some extra money.'"

Sue told me about some of the dancers that, on their nights off, walk the streets and prostitute. These girls would rather work the bar and meet "friends." Sue said that "not all of the dancers are streetwalkers but all are some sort of hooker. For a few extra dollars at a lap dance, the guy can suck, bite, kiss, and lick your tits. Some girls will let the guy finger them while the girl sits with them. The girl will stay as long as the guy keeps buying them drinks." Just then a dancer walks by. Sue said to me, "See that slut! She fucks a guy in the corner. We call her 'Red Light Chrissy.'"

I was told that there are other ways for a dancer to earn extra money while at work. These include "giving a blow job in the booths for $10.00," "dry fucks" (which is just like sex but you have all your clothes on) or "sitting with a guy and rubbing his dick until he cums." Besides working the street, doing birthday parties after work is another good way of making some extra money. Sometimes at these parties a girl is asked if she wants to have sex with a person for some more money.

I asked if there is anything that she hates about the type of job that she does. The one thing that she hates is the kind of men that come there. "They are assholes. But even so, I'll take their money and listen to their bullshit." There are a few gay women at the bar, and Sue said that one time one of them made a pass at her by pinning her against the bathroom wall: "I shoved her and told her to get away."

Little love is lost between the girls. Sue advised me not to trust my boyfriend with any of these dancers because she has seen lots of the dancers leave with someone else's boyfriend or husband. "These bitches will stab you in the back for a fuck," she said. "If you got mad about it, they would act like you did something wrong."

What are the motives for these actions? I found that a major motive was the money that can be earned. Given the limited hours and the skills that the dancers have (Sue, for example, dropped out of high school when she was 15-years-old), this is a way to make good money. "I don't know any other way of making a living," says Sue, "so I make the best of what I got." During our interview she had leave to go do a lap dance. As Sue put it, "Money is money, ya know!"

A related motive is drugs. Many of the dancers are very heavily into drugs. They work all night dancing just to go spend it all on drugs that night. They show up at work to earn more money to buy more drugs. The cycle is endless and hard to break. Some girls seek help to break this cycle, only later return and get right back into the pattern from which they just escaped.

But there are often deeper reasons in these girls' lives that are part of any explanation of what they do. Many of them come from broken homes. Their home life is full of abuse. Many of the girls are forced to prostitution either by their boyfriends, or by their spouse. In most cases the girls are subjected to physical, as well as mental abuse at home. When they come to work, this is the time of their day that men are not hurting them. Dancing is their way of getting love and tenderness—even though it is artificial and temporary.

Sue gave some insight into how she copes with the inner conflict and the thoughts that go through her head when she dances. She explains that, "The person up on stage is not really me, but my twin sister. The customers are not really there. The guy deserves to be taken advantage of, or he would not be there." She says that her actions are bad sometimes but she knows it and is the first to admit it. So this makes her better than many other people in the world because they will never admit it. They just pass the blame on to someone else.

Cyberporn
by Tyrone Good

While legitimate uses of the Internet as a tool to educate, conduct business and for recreation are being utilized, an ever-growing sub-culture seems to be saturating "the Net" with sexual solicitations, pornography, and smut designed to satisfy a whole list of fetishes. One search engine, *Yahoo*, was forced to drop its category dealing with erotica because of the system's inability to handle the overwhelming number of inquiries once they were listed!

There are rules for use that online services expect members to follow that attempt to govern sexually suggestive behavior. *America Online* has even been forced to kick members off their service for sexual offenses outlined in their terms of service manual. However, this is merely a formality because members usually sign on in the name of a family member. Much of the concern focuses on children's access and child pornography. One development of such concern is software such as *Surfwatch*, designed to create a barrier between the user's browser and the Internet, enabling parents to block out sites that are not recommended. However, children are seen as more computer literate than their parents and have discovered ways to circumvent such software!

In order to overcome the technological difficulties present when attempting to view cyberporn, which requires lots of memory to display moving nude images, CD ROM technology has been employed. This allows a user to become actively involved with actual pornographic images. For example, a user through menu options may order the image of a fully clothed woman laying poolside, to become nude, dive in the pool or simply say hello; all this and she doesn't require dinner and a movie. According to the estimates, this technology gave computer erotica a 20 percent share of the CD ROM business with sales of up to $260 million. One commentator has observed that previously X-rated pornography available only in sleazy side streets became as easy to get as ordering a pizza.

Another way that many cyberporn consumers get their smut is through computer chat rooms where sexual deviants from all over the world can live out their fantasies in the comfort of an office or their own bedroom. In order to explore this possibility I assumed a personal member profile as a "normal" college student interested in studying the prevalence of Internet sex for a college deviance course. I first entered a chat room entitled "Ask a Lesbian Anything." I asked boldly if anyone was interested in helping a college student with a research paper. I was initially confronted with skepticism by some of the ladies, but I overcame this by gaining the trust of the woman who seemed to have the most to say to the other women. After chatting about certain sexual acts, one of the women reluctantly granted me an interview in a personal chat room. Needless to say, this technique of being "friendly" would be one that I would stick to based on the subjects and myself having positive rapport, with both parties, I believe, benefitting. After deciding that I would assume the name of "Taldarkman" I continued on my journey into the underworld otherwise known as the member-created chat rooms:

Puggles: What is it that u need?
Taldarkman: Ok let me preface this by saying that this a school project—
(Professor Henry, do I get downgraded for letting her know my agenda?)

Puggles: Well I don't believe u but that is ok. (She doesn't even believe me!!!)

Taldarkman: Well that's ok. I won't ask anything out of the ordinary.

Puggles: Ok.

Taldarkman: Have you ever met someone from the net in person?

Puggles: NO! I am married, and I only get online to talk and meet people.

Taldarkman: Does your husband know of this?

Puggles: The person that I am married to is a woman

Taldarkman: OHHH!!!!!

Puggles: Yes I am very happy

Taldarkman: Well sorry for assuming

Puggles: That's fine !!! I am use to it

Taldarkman: You didn't meet your spouse online did you?

Puggles: No. A blind date

Taldarkman: Are you often solicited for sexual acts from those on the net?

Puggles: No I DON'T cyber!!! First of all that is very stupid and how can u have sex like that!! Please I love my wife and THE REAL THING!!!!!

Taldarkman: AMEN!!!

Taldarkman: Is your relationship one that is overt and known to family members friends etc.??

Puggles: YES BOTH OF OUR FAMILIES KNOW!!! IT IS REALLY NICE AND PEACEFUL

Taldarkman: Well that seems to stray from what I would expect. You are fortunate to have some understanding family members and friends

Puggles: NO OUR FAMILIES ARE VERY INTELLIGENT AND VERY LOVING AND CARING PEOPLE. AMEN TO THAT!!! YES I AM BLESSED!!!!!

Taldarkman: Well thanks for your time and since you don't believe me, when Professor Henry gives me an "A" on the paper I will be sure to send you an e-mail with the paper in its entirety.

Puggles: THANKS !!!!! HAVE A GOOD DAY!!!

Another room that caught my interest was "Dominant and Submissive Chat." I immediately looked for Marv Albert upon entering! The minute I entered the room I was solicited for cybersex by a member who stated that she was a professional woman who wanted to do a little "homework" of her own and I was the subject! Immediately realizing that this was my big break I accepted her request and it wasn't half bad!

Deciding what types of things to say was a more difficult task. I wanted to have fun, but I also wanted to maintain a certain degree of tastefulness that would keep the chat room women happy. While talking to these women, the major thing that struck me was the ease with which these people volunteered information. Confidentiality was not as requested as I thought it would be.

Many of the people that I met online had built up considerable longevity in relationships with their Internet counterparts. For instance, one room I entered was entitled "Las Vegas Swingers." Though there were 40 people in the room they immediately noticed me as an outsider. When I explained that I was a college student looking to have fun, I was told that I could gain an inside view only if I agreed to consider meeting an escort supplied by them and if she was appealing enough I would have to fork over the $1,300 nightly fee. I agreed and she was at my room in no time. Her name was Cynthia and she was strikingly attractive and gave me the old one about doing this to pay her way through college. When I told her that I honestly had no interest in her body (not for $1,300!) but that I wanted to ask her questions she was very accommodating, but at a price! I would have to allow her to use my laptop to set up her next appointment. This she said would allow her to make up for the lost time I was causing her. Would I be an accessory? Suppose she is the police? Boy did I need help! And suddenly I remembered a story I learned in my deviance class about the underworld of stolen and black-market goods in which the professor participated despite the danger. I then asked her a variety of questions about cybersex and I'm flattered to say that I think she began to like me! This raised another question. Was she simply answering me in a fashion that catered to my convenience? She offered me a chance to accompany her on one of her "routes." I declined, to her dismay, and the visit ended.

As in the "real world" not everyone that I spoke with was limited to this deviant behavior. For instance, there was the case of one individual named "Gayambass" who was a well-respected church member who explained to me that "his good deeds in the church youth group" far exceed the amount of time and energy he spends seeking prospective sex partners in the Internet chat rooms. And the facility that allows Internet accounts to have up to five screen names allows those people who have gained a bad reputation to switch to another name and a whole new personality. Gayambass has another name that allows him to make conference calls and chat with fellow church members without their knowledge of his hidden identity: "I can talk to my sex partners in one minute and in the next I will be speaking to the congregation about Bible study."

Most of the individuals that I chatted with tended to be more open-minded than society in general. My new "friends" were condemning the rest of us as robots who were either afraid or not versatile enough to engage in the behaviors they found to be second nature. In the case of "Kansaldo" who was a dominant mistress, she said that she was only exercising her true right as a woman to exceed the sexual limitations placed on her by a "closed-minded society." She went on to say that she influenced her daughter to do the same, so when she gets of age she will be free of the restrictions that a patriarchal society places on her.

Chapter 3
Restaurant Scams

Working as a server/waitstaff is one of the most common jobs performed by college students. These next four accounts describe what it is like to wait tables and how easy it is to find new and deviant ways to make money and receive free food.

The first two articles by Linda and Suzie reveal another side of the deviancy construction process by describing what has become known as the theory of office. In the course of attempting to maximize their tips, they show how waitresses and waiters create deviant customers through their use of stereotypical categories. For Linda and her fellow student servers, classifications are more often of people than of property. In Linda's restaurant, customers are stereotyped according to whether they are likely to be good or bad tippers. Deviant designation is based upon a range of psychological scans and behavioral cues to do with dress, demeanor, speech and eye contact. Similarly, Suzie says that analyzing patrons is one of the responsibilities of waiting tables. There are several types of patrons that go out to eat but they each tip differently. The criteria used to distinguish these different types include dress, race, age and sex. Once you can master the technique of distinguishing whether the patron is a "tipper" or a "stiffer," then the real money comes flowing in.

Both accounts explain that the extent to which customers receive reasonable service depends upon how they are classified and on the student's mood. "Non-tippers" are classified as deviant because they do not know how to tip; they are given a rough time, and hurried through the restaurant in order to get them replaced by "normal customers," those who "know how to tip." These classifications are justified on the basis of allowing the student server to manage the work without "going insane"

45

from the failure of customers to treat them as people and recognize their needs. Importantly, both Linda's and Suzie's articles show how deviant classifications coincide with conventional stereotypical categories that are, in part, shaped by structural stratification such as class, race and gender.

The next two articles go into more detail about how to receive "free" food and make "extra" money by "fiddling" (a British term referring to various workplace scams in which money, goods and services are obtained through concealment and guile). Gina believes that part of the server's responsibilities include deviant fiddles, which are necessary in order to make it into the waitstaff sub-culture. A server starts off as a "rookie," a role in which little is known about fiddling. But as time goes by, new employees learn the tricks of the trade from other employees and begin to cut corners to make their jobs easier and more rewarding. They graduate from "rookies" to "old-timers." Once they join the old-timers' sub-culture, they will fiddle on almost anything that seems possible.

Lisa's account on "Sidework" describes how earning a little "on the side" is a common occurrence at her restaurant called The Coach House. The main reason or motivation justifying fiddles in the minds of the servers is they feel the restaurant owes them something for their dedication and the fiddles are compensation for the low pay that they receive. Waitstaff also believe that they should be compensated when business is too slow. When management does not oblige, the waitstaff retaliates by committing fiddles. One such fiddle is networking with the cooks to receive free food. In return, the servers will do favors for the cooks. Another fiddle is to "throw away" checks at the restaurant's Sunday brunch to earn extra money.

The neutralization techniques of claim to normality, denial of victim and denial of injury are commonly used in restaurant scams. In Linda's account all of the veteran waitstaff are looking at customers' physical appearance, and particularly at their dress, in order to classify them. If you don't classify, you could be seating a couple of stiffers at your table. As Gina states, "If everyone does it, then I'm missing out by not doing it." In addition, Gina believes that a discount of fifty percent for employee meals is unreasonable, therefore her employer is seen as a "criminal" by charging her for meals. As such, the employer is the offender, not the victim (denial of victim), which frees Gina from any moral qualms about eating but not paying for "customer free" food, such as bread sticks, soup, salad, and desserts. Gina also believes that since customers receive these items in unlimited quantity, and half the time they waste most of it, then why can't she eat it for free, since no one will know and no one will get hurt (denial of injury). In addition, Lisa shows that employees use the neutralization technique of condemning the condemners, explaining that management often does the very same things that they are accused of doing, such as requesting cooks to make them dinner.

Both Suzie's and Lisa's accounts indicate the centrality of cooperative social relations among restaurant coworkers. These are not only important to sustain the informal exchange of favors, but serve as a basis for an informal subculture that has the power to control who is in and who is out. As Suzie shows, those who do not fit or whose behavior is found unacceptable are sanctioned and may ultimately be fired.

Each of these accounts illustrates that there is an art to waiting tables, whether it is typecasting the customers, finding ways to make extra money, or eating unpaid food. The students' use of various techniques of neutralization justifies their actions, partly freeing them from pangs of conscience and partly motivating their continued participation in these deviant practices. At the same time, they are linked through a subculture of informal economic activity in which each is dependent on the other and those who do not fit are forced to leave.

Waiting for Tips
by Linda Miller

For the past 26 months I have been employed as a server in a restaurant which employs 45-65 servers depending upon the season. The full complement of staff is 100 in the off-season which rises to 150 during the summer. A total of six managers are working year round.

The entire purpose of any one server is based on the assumption that diners will give an average 15% tip. A delicate balance exists between the server and diner. With an increase of the tab the level of trust increases, as do our expectations of a higher tip congruent with the tab. Servers work tables in order to increase their tip. If you don't get 20% then you feel you've not done a good job or the table just doesn't know how to tip. Those that leave less than 15% are real pains. But there is more to it than the money. As Jessica, who has worked at the restaurant for two years said, "Sure it's quick money. But it's a job that requires skills that I have. The money is good and I can make my own schedule so that I can still spend time with my family." For Tanya, who is a married college student, the money helps pay bills but she also likes the opportunity to meet different types of people and extend this into friendly relationships. Lauren, another server, feels that some of management adopt the attitude that "the customer is always right." This leads them to ignore the feelings of the staff, which gives rise to a lack of respect for the manager and a decline in the attitude and feelings of self-worth of the server.

The degree of personal satisfaction we get comes, in large part, from how we can "play" the customers, despite the restaurant rules. We are all dressed the same, follow the same rules and are present to please you, the guest. In order to combat this and in order not to blend in to the surroundings, we utilize a number of devices. The most important of these concerns stereotyping guests as they come into the restaurant.

This was Lauren's first job waiting tables and she did not even know about stereotypes prior to coming here: "I just thought the bad tips were because of my service. After I'd been here about three months I felt comfortable enough to complain about tips. Then someone started telling me about stereotypes." Now Lauren works the system of stereotypes to increase both her tips and the feeling of having done a good job. She looks at customers' physical appearance and particularly at their dress in order to classify them. She feels that if someone is dressed well and presents themselves accordingly, then they will have too much pride not to tip: "I also look at how receptive they are, their smile, their body language. Eye contact is important too. Usually that helps your tip a lot. It shows that you're paying attention. I try to make sure I don't place myself over their extended boundary. If I do they may become offended and I have to work that much harder for my tip, and there isn't always a lot of time." Lauren has low expectations of tips from customers. By underrating people she can stay happy. She is very satisfied if she gets more than she expects. She reasons that she has done a good job and maybe the guest did not generally tip that well and she was worth the tip she got.

Jessica agreed that dress was important as an indication of the kind of customer she was dealing with. She said that the manner of dress showed whether the person cared enough about themselves to spend money. Speech distinguished those who had been educated and those who had not. She said that ethnicity and social upbringing told her whether the person would know what a tip was. She felt that working in this restaurant had prejudiced her due to the way she was treated by the large number of blacks who dined there frequently. Jessica said that many were simply not aware of the concept of tipping or they "liked to be waited on by white people so that they can put us down." The tables that she had classified as non-tippers were dealt with by attempting to keep the check average low and by speeding up the service so that they could be rushed out and she could be given new customers, hopefully ones "who know how to tip."

Tanya thinks that stereotyping and the resulting exclusion of those who are unable to speak and to represent themselves is necessary and justified: "I realize that I am judging people, but that is just so that I can find an effective way of dealing with them. After all, I wait on hundreds of people. You have to label them somehow or you'll go crazy." She knows that it is not one hundred percent accurate but with practice you can get very good: "It's not possible to predict what someone will do. I can't stand it when they judge me. But I wait on people more times than any of them go out to eat. I sure can judge them a lot better than they can judge me. Besides it's my job to serve them and not theirs to guess what I'm doing."

In general Tanya goes out of her way to avoid those guests who appear to be overly curious and demanding and prefers serving men to women: "Men are more easy-going because they are in the restaurant to enjoy themselves. Women are pickier because they are used to serving their husbands and expect the same from you as they extend to their family."

For my part, I sometimes treat waiting tables as a challenge but most of the time I want my money and perform the least amount of work allowable to get it. My stereotyping is affected by my mood. When I really enjoy my work I kill every table with kindness. I carry conversations with my guests, joking, laughing. Most of the time they reciprocate and that's all that's needed. Sometimes I border on obnoxiousness to see how much I can get away with and I really enjoy it when they come back at me with their banter. This has led to the return of customers, which I guess is a goal that many of us strive for. When I'm not in my best frame of mind I just let my tables have it. Sometimes the only label a table deserves is that they are "pains." When a table has a seventy dollar order and leaves a two dollar tip, that can really set you up badly for the rest of the night.

Tippers and Stiffers
by Suzie Sullivan

I have been involved in the restaurant business for seven years. In my experience most people enter this business because of the money that can be made for relatively easy work. A secondary benefit is that they enjoy meeting new people and the jobs are typically close to home and have convenient hours. There are also several disadvantages. The job takes a lot of effort. Besides the obvious work of lifting heavy trays, memorizing menus and prices, and running around a lot, the most hazardous part of the job is meeting some customers who are infuriating pains. An unconscious part of the job is analyzing patrons. Once we have learned the job, this becomes second nature and is necessary to satisfy both the customer and ourselves. We have several stereotypes that are built on our initial assessment of patrons. Most of these types are based on dress, race, age and sex and have to do with whether the patron is a "tipper" or a "stiffer."

Where dress is concerned there are two main types. One is the shabbily dressed type—maybe a biker, rock band type with liquor-logoed t-shirts that are ripped, worn and tight, and faded jeans, tight for women and baggy for men, usually because their gut or butt is pushing them down. In this area these are typically Ypsi-tucky, hillbillies, or bikers. Attached to this stereotype is "poor tipper." Well-dressed patrons, in contrast, generally tip well. However, this is affected by race. Generally, blacks are considered bad tippers, and not only that but they make the waitress run around a lot. Orientals, in contrast, tip well and are very gracious.

Like race, age also makes a big difference. Young teens are known to be bad tippers and are harder to wait on. Part of this is because they tend to order separately on different tickets, order the cheapest item on the menu and then sit forever at your table. At one restaurant where I work they ordered a 90 cent basket of bread sticks and a lot of water. This doesn't provide for a large tab and takes valuable time running back and forth for bread and water and displaces what could be a good tipping patron. Also elderly patrons tend to be poor tippers, but they are usually pleasant to wait on.

The sex of the patron is also a factor with men generally tipping better than women, unless the woman is also a waitress. Finally, large groups are notoriously bad tippers. Part of this has to do with concern over the individual patron's personal contribution to the bill, but part also has to do with the anonymity of the group. Because no one in the group can be singled out as a tipper or a stiffer, no one feels the personal obligation to tip that they would feel if they had been sitting alone. They do not have the fear of being condemned by their peers or the server as a non-tipper.

Some of these types become apparent with experience, while others are learned from other waitresses. It is not only fun to type people but it gives the waitress a better idea of how to deal with the patron and what to expect from them, which results in making us better servers.

One aspect of the good waitress is how she conceals her personal troubles to put on an act of happy, polite and pleasurable for the table. Waitresses remark that they might come to work with a lot of problems and be in a rushed, angry and snippy mood, but when they get to that first table the cheery, bubbly, friendly personality is turned on. As one waitress told me: "You have to be up. No one wants to be served by someone mean. Besides, it helps to get a better tip." However, this is not always the case. Sometimes you can give great service, kindness, politeness, respect, a good meal, quick service and then get an insultingly low tip. This makes waitresses angry and disappointed.

In my experience, typing of customers is less a deliberate, calculated and manipulative technique to obtain better tips than it is a subconscious awareness that enables the waitress to survive and to do an effective job. It also makes the job more enjoyable.

Good waitressing also requires effort on an inner front. The sounds of restaurant work during a rush are filled with different servers asking each other to do this or that because they are so behind. If they don't get those favors done by others, they most likely would not succeed in doing their jobs. Cooperation among servers is crucial. If one doesn't get on well with the other staff members, the waitress may not survive long at an establishment.

There are usually key workers at every establishment who can arrange the termination of a coworker. All they have to do is badmouth a disliked newcomer to a manager and it can be curtains. We had one back-stabbing, two-faced, gossip-monger join us. The dining room manager and I were very close and she respected my opinion. So I made this point to talk badly about this server, based on the real stuff she was doing. On one occasion when this waitress didn't show up for one of her shifts, and didn't call until four hours after she should have been there with one of the worst excuses I've heard, I played on the fuel she provided to get her fired. The next day she was fired. It wasn't the mere incident that got her fired, since others have done the same and worse. But because of her attitude and past behavior she hadn't won the support of her coworkers and that was it.

Inner relations with the other staff can also be effective in removing a fellow worker who is disliked. I saw one girl run out on a shift sobbing because one of the key workers was giving her a bad time. When asked why she had run out, the worker innocently explained to the manager that she couldn't handle the rush.

Having good relations among staff is also imperative to get the perks of waitressing. One must have ties with the kitchen to get free food, the bar to get free drinks, managers to get the freedom to get away with it, and other staff to keep their secrets. Without these ties it is almost impossible to gain "added extras." Favors are a matter of reciprocation. They are won if you can return them at some point. If you have little to bargain with, the chances are you won't receive much. I have found that, excluding managers, the bartender has the most powerful position in a restaurant. They are the ones who can give a drink away at minimal risk owing to the fact that they are largely unsupervised. Giving a drink away to a kitchen person will entitle a bartender to a free meal or to take food home. Giving a drink to a waitress will entitle the bartender to a better tip, or free food on a night off. Giving a free drink to a patron entitles the bartender to a better tip, as well as some insurance that the patron will come again.

The waitress doesn't have much bargaining power because she has very little to offer the other restaurant workers that they can't already get. The only power they have is over the customer. The only time they give stuff away to customers is when someone they know comes in. The primary motive here is to be nice, and to show kindness towards their friend, family, teacher or acquaintance. The goal of being motivated by a bigger tip is a secondary consideration, although in these circumstances, more time, not a bigger tip is received.

Although trading free food and drinks is most common, other activities include stealing silverware or glasses and overcharging the customer. These are less common because control systems, especially computers, make this more difficult. In some establishments that do not use a computer system, overcharging can be rife, systematically a dollar or more per order, especially on drinks.

Deviant activities such as these are an accepted part of the restaurant business and become second nature to the employee. Most employees feel that stealing is morally wrong but that what goes on at work is different. Waitstaff believe that because they work at an establishment they are owed these things and everyone there does it. However, for the most part, this sub-culture of restaurant life does not sustain large thefts; nor, for that matter, does it cultivate the conniving, dishonest, or sneaky individual but rather a cooperative crew of employees who deviate to keep their work flowing and their problems at a minimum.

Pasta Anyone?
by Gina Stafford

I work at the Pasta Pavilion restaurant. The most common form of employee deviance is stealing food. At the Pasta Pavilion, the policy on food consumption states that any food eaten must be paid for prior to consumption. Employees receive a discount of fifty percent; however, most think this is somewhat unreasonable. One server I interviewed stated, "I do feel we should be charged for entree items, but stuff like bread sticks, soup, salad, and desserts should be free. After all, customers receive these items in unlimited quantity, and half the time they waste most of it." This person then confessed to eating at least one bowl of soup or a bread stick per shift without paying for it. She also claimed that whenever possible, she would write up tickets for entrees and later void them out. If questioned, a simple "Oh, I lost or threw out that ticket," would suffice. By claiming that customers receive free unlimited refills, this employee is justifying her actions by reference to a sense of justice or equal treatment. This employee also stated that everyone else seems to do it, so why shouldn't she? This seems to be a widely held belief in our establishment, in which it is stated, "Everybody steals from their employer."

The second type of deviance at the Pasta Pavilion is making extra money. This is very common because employees tend to feel that they have the right to more money. A few of the employees I interviewed basically displayed the same attitude. One told me, "Waiters and waitresses only make $2.52 an hour. I realize we also get tips, but some customers seem to think we make a killing. This may be true on a Friday or Saturday night, but I'm lucky if I average $3.00 an hour for working lunch. I personally feel that we should get paid at least minimum wage, the same as all other employees."

It is plain to see why making extra money is such a common practice. Employees feel it is only fair given their low pay. One employee explained how the practice takes place: "Whenever I take an order for any food item which does not have to be sent to the back line (to the cook), I write it on a separate sheet of paper. I wait until after it is printed out, and then I add it in on the top copy that the office gets (our tickets are computerized). Instead of turning in the entire check, I pocket the amount of money the customer gave for the whole check. The office never knows because they are unaware what the customer ordered." This practice is frequently used during the lunch hours, due to the fact that this is when most people order soup, salad, and bread sticks (an order costing $4.95). This type of order does not get sent to the cook. It is seen by the server and the customer only. The server hand-writes the check, the customer pays for it, and the check is then torn up. The Pasta Pavilion does not require employees to account for their tickets.

I questioned many employees about this activity. The rookies were ignorant to it, whereas the "old-timers" were well aware of it. This difference is explained by the fact that as time goes by, employees become more in tune to what other employees are doing. I feel another reason for rookies' ignorance is that new employees tend to follow the rules but, little by little, they begin to cut corners to make their jobs easier, more interesting, and more rewarding. I found that for money, employees are willing to scam on almost anything. There seems to be a certain "hype" employees get from stealing. The general attitude seems to be that, "If everyone does it, then I'm missing out by not doing it."

Sidework
by Lisa Lockhart

I am employed as a waitress at a local restaurant, The Coach House. At this restaurant employees daily engage in various activities that are deviant and to some extent criminal. In particular they subvert the system of perks that allows them discounted meals. One of the most frequent ways to do this is for waitstaff to fail to ring in items on the computer, but to somehow manage to serve these items. There are several ways in which this can be accomplished. One is to ask the kitchen or bar staff to supply the items needed in return for a favor later, or as a token of friendship. This type of activity is of a casual nature. The waitstaff either restricts this practice to items over which they have control, such as soup, salads, soft drinks, or to inexpensive items, like asking the cooks to add an extra topping on the pizza. Those employees tend not to abuse this benefit and use it wisely to their advantage.

Some employees, however, get carried away with greed. At The Coach House there has been a recent rash of excessive deviant behavior during the Sunday brunch. The Coach House uses a computer system to order food and drinks and prints checks to present to customers for payment to the waitstaff for their meal. Each waitstaff member is provided with an individual key with which they can access the computer, and in turn, are responsible for payment to the restaurant for all charges on that key. During Sunday brunch several members of the waitstaff have discovered that many of their tables are a consistent size and have a tendency to order the same items; two Sunday brunches and two coffees for example. The waiter enters the items into the computer in order to present the bill to the customer. Once the waiter enters this information into the computer he can recreate a check several times and present it to different tables as their personal check. This waiter then collects the money from the customers but only has to pay the restaurant for one check since the computer only has a record of the one check entered in it. At the end of the Sunday brunch shift it is estimated that those waiters who do this go home with an extra one to two hundred dollars.

This type of activity has been frequent enough for management at The Coach House to become alarmed. Lori, the general manager, became aware of this problem through casual conversation with employees from a different and separate restaurant that has no association with our own. Lori said, "I can't believe this is happening." In this case it is not a matter of management looking the other way. After this problem was brought to management's attention there was an immediate investigation. Since management quietly looked into the matter, those waitstaff members engaged in this activity who did not curtail their deviant behavior proceeded to get caught.

The computer system has a record of all checks printed in its memory. All management has to do is get copies of the checks that were printed and match them with the record of guests received by the hostess. The result of this investigation caused the termination of one employee, Stu. Not knowing Stu had been released from his position at The Coach House, I spoke with him about a schedule change, at which time he informed me he had been fired for what he lead me to believe was no apparent reason, or at least unjustified. It was later learned at an employee meeting that Stu had recreated a guest check 22 times and collected for each of those bills but only turned in one amount, pocketing the rest. The reaction to this announcement was one of shock that Stu would steal so much from the restaurant. Stu is still considered to be a nice guy by a lot of the employees but also very stupid for he "didn't know when enough is enough." I was unable to speak with Stu after receiving this information but upon listening to speculation by other employees as to why he did this, they couldn't figure it out.

As a result of this incident, Sunday brunch is not an enjoyable shift to work for many employees because they are under such severe scrutiny by management. The employees understand management's sudden strictness but it still makes them feel "untrustworthy" when management scrutinizes the day's receipts as if the employees are hard-core criminals.

The Coach House, in its attempts to subsidize the low basic rate of pay, offers non-tipped employees free meals after 6 hour shifts if the meals they choose are under $5.00 or they are to pay 50% of all menu items that are more expensive. The 50% off all menu items is the policy for all tipped employees. Although employees get discounts on food, they seem to cheat on their meals. It is a common practice for the waitstaff to walk into the kitchen and ask a cook to make their dinner. The kitchen staff, knowing full well that they are not supposed to make any meals without a printout from the computer, usually makes the meals for the staff anyway.

I spoke to members of the kitchen staff about this practice and if they followed it. One of the line cooks, Sam, told me he made the meals for employees at the rate of approximately 10 a day. When I asked why he did this, he said he did it "just because" and could not think of an answer to justify his actions for me. But Sam did state that he regulates how often he does this and points out that he doesn't always comply with coworkers' requests for food because "they ask too often, some of them every day." I also interviewed a waitress, Jo, about how often she makes a request for food and why. She told me she didn't always ask for free food but when she did, it was usually after an extremely slow or busy shift. She justified this by the fact that during slow times she did not make any money in tips and the hourly rate was ridiculously low, proving to herself that "the restaurant owes me this." She also used the same justification that the "restaurant owes me" after working a busy shift in which she was unable to take a break or was forced to deal with an unusual amount of stress during her shift. When suggesting that the failure to ring in her own meal was a crime, she did not consider it so for she had witnessed the same type of deviant behavior from management. When asked to explain this, I was informed that management also had a tendency to request food without ringing the items up even though they are able to write the meals off. Jo also spoke about management control of these fiddles, especially if she was caught asking the kitchen staff to make her dinner. She explained that she would ring a meal in to evade any punishment. She felt that those who had been caught were just unlucky or too stupid to know when not to take items from the restaurant.

In some cases, no matter how careful an employee is about not getting caught fiddling or how little they do this, they are always the ones to get caught. I was involved in one such incident. I had asked the pizza cook to make a pizza for my personal consumption and to put the pizza in my car for me, to avoid detection by management. Management saw the pizza and I had to own up to my deviant behavior. The punishment I received was to pay full price and to be put on probation for 30 days. At the time I felt anger towards the restaurant, mostly because I felt they owed me something and I felt I should not have had to pay for something I felt I rightfully deserved. As time has passed I now realize that I was in the wrong, but also believe the restaurant owes me something for my long dedication to the establishment.

To summarize, in my experience earning "a little on the side" seems common in the restaurant business and the idea that employees receive food as a benefit for their time and effort appears to be acceptable up to a point. At The Coach House, it was revealed that cooks didn't cheat all the time for everyone who asked, but kept it to a limit. One of the main reasons for the cheating was a belief that the restaurant owed them that little bit for the dedication to the restaurant and for the low pay which they received. At The Coach House, employees (especially waitstaff) believed that they should be compensated if it was too slow. In almost all these cheating situations there is a need for cooperation between two or more people; for instance, the waitress needs the cook to prepare the food for her. The cook in return may ask for a favor later on.

For their part the management generally looks the other way in order to appease their employees. This gives the employees reinforcement for their justifications. Through interviews and observations I came to realize that the management at The Coach House is, to some extent, respected by the staff. As a result of this respect the employees voluntarily cut down on their cheating, especially when management is going through rough periods.

Chapter 4
Deviance at Work

In the previous section we focussed on a special case of deviance in the workplace involving restaurant employees. Of course such activity is not restricted to restaurants and the articles in this chapter illustrate a variety of other work settings in which similar activities occur. Deviance at work often involves students taking items such as office supplies, clothes, material or food and drink from where they are employed; or it involves various scams for making money on the side. Maria's account of prostitution among nurses shows the extent to which students will go to make money from side work. The account by Carol also describes deviant workplace activities from the perspective of a hospital employee, revealing that a main motive for theft of materials and time is hating the job. Jerry, who is a student maintenance worker, explains how resentment for the company owner turns into part-time crime as employees have no respect for their boss. Here scams approximate corporate fraud as student employees are ordered to cheat (through doing poor work) their customers or clients who are themselves often other students. This serves the owner's interest in getting extra business in callbacks, and also involves deviance against the government since these students are being employed off the books to avoid taxes. The other accounts probe different dimensions of deviance at work.

Scott's account describes how mall security officers receive "discounts" from various mall employers and "tips" as a result of helping mall customers and how this relieves the boredom of an otherwise dull job. Bill's account describes overcharging the customer and committing fraud against the public. Tom shows how employee theft is routine, even in the most disciplined of settings such as the military. Tom also reveals how recruits are introduced to deviant activity by their supervisors, just as they are introduced to other aspects of the work setting. In the other accounts, more experienced student workers showed newcomers the ropes. In Jerry's account of a university housing maintenance crew, we see that the fraud actually impacts the students and is facilitated by the employer, rather than the employees, who are mere tools in his corruption.

The obvious rewards for taking others' property are either the money or the goods obtained. But these contributions show that other motives can be just as prominent. Scott shows that all the various scams of mall security officers provide an interest to the job, break the monotony and give them fun and excitement at beating the system. Scott, Jerry and Carol's accounts show that deviance is often committed because they are disgruntled employees and the deviance serves to get back at the supervisor or their employer in general (denial of victim). Workers at the hospital pilfer items because they believe that either they should not pay for items, that they are "owed" this by the hospital for all the aggravation they have to suffer (denial of victim), or that the hospital can afford it or can write it off (denial of injury). Some of Jerry's fellow maintenance workers claim that it is not their fault that shoddy work gets done but the fault of the employer who orders it so he can increase the demand for his business (denial of responsibility). For Maria, who is a student nurse at a local hospital, sex for money can be used to help "cure" the patients (appeal to higher loyalties). Here student nurses, who are gaining an education through an internship, are also conducting a side business in prostitution. But as Maria's article indicates, the business that stereotypically occurs on the street or in clubs, when conducted in the context of a therapeutic setting, can be justified as "helping the patients."

A less dramatic form of deviance at work is taking early lunches and staying longer, but the reasons for this may be no less significant than in Maria's prostitution: Bill and his fellow workers like to gamble and take drugs during lunch break.

Tom shows that while the tangible motive for employee theft is obtaining equipment in short supply, peer pressure and sub-cultural conformity are also important motives in the decision to deviate, since the students are trying to "fit in" to behavior that everyone else seems to be doing. Yet other soldiers clearly accrue status and prestige among their group for being "a supplier." This belief is also shared by Carol and her fellow workers. Stealing from the hospital is performed because it makes one feel more "powerful" that they got away with it. However, for Maria, the hospital setting provides the context that justifies nurses prostituting themselves to patients. Maria shows that for her fellow co-nurses, having sex with paying patients is no different than having the patient pay for hospital bills or medicine. Therefore, the nurse has a motive to help the patient receive "treatment" and the deviant nature of the act of prostitution becomes morally blurred.

In both Bill and Tom's accounts, deviance is often related to a structure of moral meaning. In Tom's account the acquisition of "supplies" through pilfering is positively valued by officers in the military unit. In Bill's road construction consulting company, cheating the client involves charging them excess travel and gas mileage for services. Everyone who works does the same scam, so if someone does not cheat the client then they are breaking the informal rules and will be replaced.

Similarly, the theft of military equipment is governed by informal rules which redefine what is acceptable and what is not. If a person has to go out of their way to steal, the behavior is regarded as unacceptable; but if they come by the materials in the normal course of their work, then that is seen as acceptable. Also, materials are classified according to who owns the property; theft of personal property is unacceptable and results in moral condemnation from fellow soldiers, but it is quite acceptable to take unit property and property with no apparent owner.

Other more serious crimes are also committed at work. For example, fraud against the public is present in Bill's account of road construction. Workers fix the results of compaction tests. Roadways are given passing grades so workers don't have to fix a road which would take weeks to complete. Scott and other security guards, who are supposed to be protecting the public, confiscate valuable "lost and found" items, without giving the real owners a chance to redeem their property. In the account by Jerry Built, maintenance workers make unnecessary repairs on people's homes and fraternity houses on college campuses in order to enhance profits. Repairs are done incorrectly the first couple of visits so the maintenance company can keep coming back. Because of this practice homeowners are billed excess amounts and the students are forced to live in substandard housing. Other corruption in Jerry's account includes secretaries filling out false billing papers and repairmen taking home maintenance items and taking part in time theft.

These accounts reveal that being employed involves much more than is contained in the formal job description and suggests that the real enjoyment and meaning of many jobs comes from the informal rewards, and not always to the benefit of the students themselves.

Compliments of the Hospital
by Carol Fairchild

I work as a technician performing pregnancy tests in a blood gas lab. The lab is overseen by the respiratory therapy department of a university hospital. The department oversees two small labs, the pulmonary lab and the blood gas lab. The pulmonary lab does testing for cystic fibrosis. The blood gas lab tests blood samples for premature babies, checking to see if they need assistance in breathing by the use of ventilator machines. This lab also performs pregnancy tests. Both labs give technicians access to computer equipment, life cycle machines, office and cleaning supplies, blank cassette tapes, postal supplies, typewriters, xeroxing machines, telephone services and pharmaceutical products.

Employees in the lab engage in a variety of activities, some of which simply involve stealing time, by arriving late and leaving early, while recording work time for a full day's pay of 12 hours. The technicians may also perform their tasks in less than the allotted time, freeing the rest of the day to do what they want, such as studying, writing a paper, or just goofing off. It is rare that tests are demanded immediately, but this does sometimes happen. Other deviant activities involve using the phone system to make long distance calls. Perhaps the most surprising is that pregnancy tests are performed free of charge for personal use, family, friends and coworkers. The technician may charge a small fee, which is pocketed rather than given to the institution. This is referred to by staff as "the complementary service" of the hospital. There is little discussion of these activities among the techs, but they do discuss and condemn what other staff are doing.

The university hospital setting has many rules and procedures but is not intensely managed. There are many supervisors but they are so concerned with the details of their jobs that they spend very little time watching over their employees. As long as supervisors do not receive complaints from other staff members, the workers are considered to be "on their own." There is no hierarchy of commands since all the tests are seen as equally important and all the techs are doing the same kind of work.

One employee, Jack, admits to taking home many of the materials we work with: "Let's see, I've taken batteries, rubberbands, staples and the stapler, pencils and pens. I've taken garbage bags, plastic buckets, bed sheets and pillowcases. You name it, I've got it. I even took the life-cycle machine in the pulmonary lab home, but I brought it back." Jack also uses his lunch breaks to sleep: "I usually extend our 45 minute lunch break into an hour and a half to two hours," he says. "I tried to use sick time. Remember when I was off sick for that week. I was with my girl. I even had all my calls forwarded to her house. But Jill (the supervisor) really stuck it to me bad, so I try not to use sick time. I hate hearing her mouth. She's a bitch. She never practices what she preaches." Jack says he hates the job but continues to do it because of the perks: "It's the only job I've found that pays well, where I can listen to the radio, talk on the phone, do my homework and still get paid for a 12 hour day. I actually work 4 out of 12 hours!"

Simon also admits to taking "small stuff, like alcohol pads, bottles of Tylenol and peroxide, as well as the usual stuff like computer paper, garbage bags and paper towels." But his particular favorite is making long distance calls on the lab phone. For Mary pilfering involves, "bottles of alcohol and lotion. I take those little bars of soap, just in case I run out or decide to travel. I take tubes of toothpaste, combs and brushes, liquid soap, garbage bags, toilet rolls, milk, cereal, boxes of pens and pencils for my nieces. They never have to worry about school supplies. I once took home the radio from the other lab because my car radio stopped working. But I brought it back before anyone noticed it was missing." Unlike the other two Mary seldom extends her lunch breaks: "I usually bring my lunch and eat alone." But she does take sick days: "At least once a month. Either I tell Sue I have cramps really bad or I'll disguise my voice and make it sound like I'm really sick. Besides, you don't get paid for the time you don't use, so why not take it?"

Jack offered several reasons why he pilfers materials. He says he doesn't see why he should pay for something he can get for free. Mary agrees and adds that "I'm a college student and I'm poor." In addition she has little respect for her supervisor. She says, "Sue is two-faced. She'll talk about you behind your back." Jack also says he hates his job, hates his supervisor and argues that the hospital doesn't pay him enough. He says what he takes is a "shift differential" to make up for what he doesn't get. He discounts the seriousness of his stealing by referring to the materials pilfered as "tidbits" and "nothing major, like VCRs or computers." He claims that the hospital won't miss it and that "I'm sure that whatever they find missing they can write off on their taxes or as a donation or something." Simon also adds to the justifications by pointing out that even the supervisor pilfers stuff: "I once saw her take an unopened box of computer paper home. If she wants to say something to me I won't hesitate in letting her know what I saw."

Simon is more direct, however, about the motives for his pilfering, seeing them as a direct result of the way the supervisor, Sue, and the hospital generally treat him: "I don't like her and I can take or leave the job. But I've no choice. She comes with the job. But she really never listens to our needs. She never knows what is going on in the lab until it's too late. Then when her supervisors start to shit on her, she shits on us. I don't like the job because there is no room for progress. You're on one level and that's where you stay. I feel that the way this place treats you, you should be entitled to whatever you want. The verbal and mental abuse they put you through is too much. A paycheck isn't enough to compensate for the stress you're under. It's not so much the job but the people." The general consensus is why should they care about their jobs and what they do when their employer doesn't care about them or what they do so long as they analyze the tests correctly.

Nurse-Prostitutes Giving "Treatment"
by Maria Meyer

One night, during the midnight shift, I was cleaning the hospital rooms when I walked in on a fellow nurse, my friend, Andrea. I was shocked when I saw she was giving one of my patients head! I didn't know what to do or say. I avoided Andrea until later that night. Andrea then explained, "Hospital wages are not paying my school bills or rent." She needed to find a way to make extra money, and prostitution seemed like a good idea.

I asked her if anyone else was doing this. She told me that there were three other nurses, all around the ages of 21 to 30. I knew each of these nurses. I decided to ask them separately to explain their deviant behavior.

All agreed that client selection was based on three factors: proposition by the client, medical history, and solicitation by the nurse. All the nurses received money as payment and one would accept payment in the form of drugs. None of the nurses have worked during the day shift since the time they began prostituting. Although risky, one nurse, Amy, began prostituting when she was scheduled on day shift: "If I had a client that wanted sex during the day, then I would have to come into work early. But it was a lot easier on the second shift or midnight shift, since the staff size decreases and you don't really need a look-out."

When asked about the privacy of a hospital room and if they would solicit a client who had a roommate, all participants said yes. Vickie, the oldest of the four who is not in college, explained: "That's why it is so easy on midnight shift. Their roommates are asleep. But if the roommate is up, then I simply pull the curtain."

Over the past couple of years, only one girl had been caught with a client, and the incident was written up as sexual misconduct. She was dismissed from the job, but not prosecuted. The remaining four girls believe that they are being suspected of sexual misconduct. So they act with great caution now, instead of the old "hay days" where they were not careful.

None of these nurses felt that they were engaging in deviant behavior. All of them held conventional values and had mastered rationalizations that allowed them to vacillate between conventional and deviant behavior without any stigmatizing effects, so long as they were not caught. Rationalizations included: "No one is getting hurt from our sexual activities. Hey, the hospital doesn't know, our customers are happy, and I'm happy because I now have extra cash."

"Securing" the Shopping Mall
by Scott Malone

I work in a large shopping mall as a security officer. My job is to protect mall property from loss by theft or vandalism. It is also to deter crime simply by being visible and to provide customer service when necessary.

The security department of the mall is hierarchically structured just like a police department. At the top is the security director. A lieutenant oversees supervision of the shift sergeants, who are in charge of the officers on their shift. As a patrol officer I am at the bottom of the chain of command.

I patrol the mall during my shift by walking around inside or by driving around in the parking lot in a security vehicle. I am free to roam anywhere on mall property, which gives me a great deal of autonomy, except on those occasions when I am called over my two-way radio to report somewhere. I think it would be most useful if I described for you how a typical day in security operates, "warts an' all"!

There is a twenty-four hour security presence in this mall and we work eight-hour shifts. The shifts are day ("morning") (8 AM-4 PM), afternoon (4 PM-12 AM) and the midnight shift (12 AM-8 AM). The entire management is present on the morning or day shift so things pretty much run by the book. The morning crew is responsible for answering the phones and monitoring the alarm system until the mall opens at 10 AM. The sergeant generally does some paperwork, but this rarely takes more than half an hour. Any parking tickets issued from the previous day have to be taken to the city parking department. In addition the security vehicles must be washed. Surprisingly, it is not very busy during the day and extra breaks are often taken to kill time.

The afternoon shift is the busiest of the three. Most patrons come to the mall after getting off work and they bring their families to have dinner, go shopping, and maybe see a movie. Teens also come to the mall after school to hang out with their friends. With the exception of one person, the entire management leaves for the day at 5 PM. At this time the security officers give a sigh of relief because it means they can do things their own way, without having to constantly look over their shoulders. Management seem to have this superhuman power that enables them to be everywhere at the same time and you can bet that when you screw up, one of them will be right there, which has resulted in a CYA (Cover Your Ass) doctrine among security officers.

With management gone and the mall full of shoppers things can get hectic. Shoppers lose things, have things "stolen," including their cars, which is sometimes fact, but often the result of them either forgetting where they parked it or leaving the mall through a different entrance from the one they came in. The proper procedure with lost property is to take it to a "lost and found" file in the security office. But not everything security officers come by ends up in the lost and found. If a person inquires about something and the item is not there, then as far as anyone knows, security never knew it existed. It has probably become someone's "perk of the job".

Autonomy reflected in these "extras" is very important in this job, since it allows us to break from the discipline and routine nature of the work. Basic security work is often very monotonous and various antics engaged in by security personnel add a thrill and excitement that is almost never there as part of the regular work. So patrol officers are constantly trying to create their own space for pleasure while on the job. This is done mainly by "making time." Apart from the obvious extensions of lunch hours or coffee breaks there are other things that provide freedom from boredom. For example, by getting on the good side of supervisors, you can take longer breaks and take care of personal business such as shopping, banking, and phone calls, all without catching flack or being reprimanded.

Another way of making sure that you are more controlling than controlled is through developing personal contacts among the various mall store staff. This is not only good for mall relations and for improving overall confidence of the businesses, but it comes with additional perks for the patrol officer. These include receiving free or discounted food while on the job and receiving free services, such as eye exams or merchandise repair from mall stores. Discounted food and services are very common on the afternoon shift. Many of the stores hire college students who can only work afternoons themselves. These are the people most likely to give something for nothing, especially since many of the officers are also college students and have friends who work throughout the mall. These officers know who to go to if they want something and they very seldom have to pay full price.

The mobile unit also affords the opportunity for some little extras. For example, when on external security duty the mobile patrol does many assists, especially during the afternoon. These include jump-starts and getting keys out of people's cars if they lock themselves out. Before this service is rendered a waiver must be signed by the person in need. At this time most people ask how much the charge is going to be. What they don't know is that the service is free. If the officer needs a little cash this is the perfect time to collect it! Outright lies are often not necessary, especially if you tell them that you will do this **for them,** for free. Many customers offer tips. They are only too pleased to have their car going again. Officers are supposed to refuse these gratuities, and if the customer "insists," they are to be turned in to management. But since management is usually gone, the tip rarely makes it through to them the next day. After the mall is closed at 9 PM, the only remaining duties are to lock the doors and make sure everyone is out of the mall.

This brings us to the midnight shift which is the most lax of the three. No one is there from management and required duties are limited and simple. We are required to make occasional patrols of the parking lot in the security vehicle, patrol the interior of the mall and to unlock certain doors near the end of the shift. The most important function is the interior patrols. These must be done at specified times and are documented by a series of watch clock check stations. Since two officers work this shift, they generally take turns sleeping while the other does the work. During this work it is not unknown for officers to enter the movie theaters and play video games to break the monotony.

Most of the security officers are involved in these kinds of antics at one time or another. When you first begin the job the other officers teach you the "ins and outs." They also make it known that if you don't take part you won't be accepted as part of the group. That can be quite a strong pressure, although the pressure is not really needed. After about a week of midnights, things become so boring that these "side activities" and "extras" become a kind of game to see what you can get away with. As long as it doesn't get out of hand people mind their own business.

All of these inside aspects of security, which are not formally part of the job, help to make it more interesting. When you are "at the bottom of the totem pole" you don't have much power or control, if any at all. Taking advantage of or "screwing the company over" is not only fun and challenging, it also gives a feeling of power and control to those who have none.

To my knowledge no one at this job has ever been formally prosecuted or even caught doing these things. If there was any suspicion that an employee was up to no good, the company would simply let them go. But this rarely happens because the company doesn't know anything is going on.

Most of the officers have no moral qualms about the stuff they get in to because they believe that the company "shafts" them in many ways, and that by taking things from the company they get even. I guess there is something of a revenge motive there. In the eyes of most officers they are only taking what they had worked for. The wages in this kind of work are so low that they see this as a way of making up the difference. Besides, the loss to the company is so small they don't even notice it. Ironically, these shenanigans actually help to keep the security officers happy, which keeps the operation of the mall running smoothly. We rely on the perks to keep us going. Without them the security organization would probably fail.

Theft of Military Equipment
by Tom North

Under the Uniform Code of Military Justice, theft is a criminal offense just as it is in the civilian sector; but it is not always a violation of the norms. As a member of the armed forces I am in constant contact with, and am friends of, people who pilfer military equipment. In recent times the Army has started cracking down on the theft of military equipment and many who do it are reluctant to talk. This has also caused many to be more careful when taking stock.

Both of the soldiers that I talked to started pilfering relatively early in their careers, one when he was in basic training. They said that several people they knew were doing it and one said that he was encouraged to do it: "In fact my squad leader was doing it and he got all the new guys involved." I have observed squad leaders say that any time we got a chance to take something we should do it because that would be the only way to get it. New people entering the military are constantly exposed to this kind of advise and they soon learn that it is acceptable behavior. They engage in this behavior because everyone else is doing it and they are just trying to fit in. Indeed, the older men in their mid-thirties seemed to be taking more equipment than the new recruits.

From my own experience and observations I had learned that people took equipment because it was the normal thing to do and because it is unavailable in other ways but there were other reasons as those I spoke to explained. For one thing it was taken simply because it was unguarded and easy to get. People rarely, if ever, go out of their way to get a piece of equipment; they just come by it. Although sometimes one would stand watch while another took the equipment. Other reasons given for taking equipment had to do with status and prestige within the unit. As one of the soldiers said, "Sometimes you get praised by others for being able to get equipment and have it ready when they need it. You get a reputation as a supplier."

There was a certain set of informal, taken-for-granted ways to go about pilfering. Those solders I spoke with felt that it was wrong to sell equipment but one said that he occasionally traded it with people in the same unit. Mostly the equipment is taken for personal use and for use by friends. Cleaning supplies are a good example. These are taken and put in the person's locker in the armory and distributed within the platoon when needed. Equipment was seen as one of three types: "personal property," "unit property" and "equipment that you find." There seemed to be strong informal rules against taking personal equipment: "You never take someone else's stuff because they would have to pay for it." A person who gets caught taking personal gear is looked down upon by everyone in the unit. He is seen as a despicable person and not to be trusted. In contrast, the solders generally felt that it was all right to take the unit's property, unless it was something that was on a hand receipt such as a weapon or a radio. As one said, "It belongs to the Army and they are always wasting money so who cares?" The other said, "It doesn't really hurt anyone because it doesn't belong to anyone. Anyway the supply sergeant can cover it up just by changing the paperwork." Nor was anything seen as wrong with taking equipment that was found. The belief was that the person who lost it is "going to have to pay for it anyway." Since the lost item did not really belong to anyone it was all right to take it home.

From my observations it was clear that although the officers were officially against theft, this was part of their job and was seen as such by the enlisted men, most of whom were not particularly against the behavior. Most of the people in the unit had a favorable view of those who pilfered goods, referring to them as "suppliers" who can get whatever they need. Neither of those I spoke to had been caught taking personal equipment. However, the Army's recent increase in controls had forced both the solders to go to greater lengths than before to avoid being caught. One reported that he is now so afraid of being caught that he will have to stop taking equipment. He says that he has already had to stop taking home some of the smaller things such as blank ammunition and pyrotechnics.

Crime on the Road
by Bill West

I work as an engineering consultant providing corporate clients with consultation for construction work. Our firm is hired to do special tests for construction buildings, new roadways, backfill of sewer trenches, and surveying basically anything to do with construction. Once the tests or observations are done, our firm sends the results back and recommends if the construction is satisfactory in meeting the various building standards and codes. My job is to go out on my own to construction sites and to perform compaction tests on the materials.

The way the organization is set up the employees are tempted to commit several deviant acts. In most cases the worker is basically on his own after he is assigned his duties for the day. He goes out to the construction site, meets with a supervisor or worker to find out which part of the roadway or sewer trench needs a compaction test. The materials that are tested are native soil or stone brought in for backfill of the roadway or sewer trench. We test this material by hammering a spike into the new surface, then removing the spike and inserting a rod into the hole left by the spike, which is connected to an electronic sensor device and computer which gives a reading that helps the worker determine if the new surface or material is hard enough. After this is done we tell the contractor if the material passes the test or we recommend what more has to be done if the material fails. This usually involves the client running a roller over the roadway some more times and then retesting.

One of the common scams here is to cheat the client. This might involve the worker charging the client excess travel and gas mileage. For example, if it took twenty minutes to get to the job site and thirty miles travel, we might charge thirty minutes and thirty-five miles travel. As Terry explained, "By doing this it gives me extra time, so I can relax and take time on my work, plus the extra mileage gives me extra money." He justifies this on the grounds of equity saying: "My car guzzles more than others so I'm getting a fair gas allowance."

We sometimes add extra time to the time sheet beyond what we actually work. This is especially likely to happen when the supervisor, who is usually the client, is not around. The company recommends that we work seven and a half hours for a complete day. This has to be signed off on the time charge sheet that is given to the client. We are also encouraged to have all the work charged to the client, and not have any charged to our own account. For example, we might complete tests at 3 o'clock but write up the time sheet for a 4 o'clock finish. This allows us to go home early and still get paid. As Ken says, "I do this so that I meet my daily quota, plus I can go run some errands or go sleep somewhere or even get in some extra overtime by getting another assignment." On other occasions Bobby says, "There are guys who do it when it's too hot to work, so they can go home and not have to deal with the heat."

Gambling and drug use often take place during lunchtime. We play cards such as "hearts." Gerry said, "I never thought of gambling as bad. I guess it's ok to do it. Since I've been working here cards have always been played at lunch." Ben, the supervisor, explained the card playing, saying, "It's only petty gambling. Besides, it boosts morale among the workers, and something is said if it gets out of hand."

Some of the workers are into drugs but no one really says anything about it. There are only four to eight guys who smoke pot. That leaves eight others who don't get involved in the drug scene. At times there are workers who get high before work or who even step out during work to burn a joint. One worker explains why he does it: "I like it. Sometimes during work it gets boring so I ask whoever's around, usually close friends, if they want to go out and burn one. This makes the day go by faster and work is not so boring." It seems to keep the employees in good spirits. Reflecting on the drug use, the supervisor says, "I know there's guys who do drugs. As long as I don't see them using them or working under the influence and the job gets done, there's no problem." One worker who does not do drugs commented, "It's their business, as long as they keep control. I haven't seen anything get crazy yet."

Clearly, gambling and drug use result in some time loss to the company and inefficient work, but this is not its primary motive. Indeed, it may actually increase productivity and efficiency since it keeps morale high.

Another form of deviance at work is people coming in late and taking early lunches or long ones during which they will get in some extra gambling and step out to get high. Ken says, "There is usually no one around most of the time to check how late we get back from lunch. If I come in late, I just work later to make up for the time I missed. You just got to be careful and as long as you get your full day in, it's ok." The supervisor comments on the lateness. He says, "They're just hurting themselves. Being late usually results in getting shitty assignments or no assignment at all, causing them to hang around the lab to clean up or else I'll find them something real hard to do if their lateness becomes a habit."

A more serious crime is fraud against both the client and indirectly against the public. We might conduct the compaction test and then calculate the results. It's required to test the new roadway every 10 meters. Cheating comes about because after conducting a few tests on different areas of the road, and finding that these pass, the employee will then make up test locations and readings for the remaining road surface. The roadway would be given a passing grade, although only five official tests were made compared with the 10 written in the report. As Bobby says, "Basically, if there are several areas that pass there's a 90% chance that the rest of the roadway will pass." He explains, "If a problem does arise, it's not usually noticeable until after a few months. It's just like gambling. The odds are in your favor if you use the right judgment."

Usually, if a problem arises, like a pothole or asphalt breaking up on a new roadway, the client would first check the test results. If the problem is in the test area, further checking is done. The supervisor explains that the next thing that happens is "We get our big people with the clients. If it comes down that one of our employees is at fault, he is usually fired or given a good talking to. It all depends on how severe the problem is." Some workers accept this type of punishment. As Ken says: "Well, I guess it's fair to get fired if it's a big problem. There can be a serious lawsuit if a driver gets in an accident due to a defect on a road."

The supervisor believes that the reason why there is so much rule-breaking is because of the unsupervised nature of the work: "We keep track of those who screw around. If it gets out of hand we usually give them bullshit jobs and if it keeps up we talk to him, give him warnings. It's basically like baseball: three strikes and you're out!"

I believe that in addition to the lack of supervision you also pick up ways of making an extra buck and how not to work your ass off. As Ken explains: "Our company is not actually paying us. It's the client, usually the city and they've got all kinds of money."

"Fixing" University Housing
by Jerry Buildt

I work for a company that is contracted by The University to repair student housing. Maintenance workers make repairs on the fraternity houses and also do modernization work in people's homes. I am employed as a maintenance worker for the company. The student fraternity houses, most of which are over 100-year-old landmark homes, require maintenance but because of the way we are told to do the work, they have to be repaired several times over. If the repairs were done correctly in the first place the company would make less money and would need less maintenance men. Because of this practice, owners of the homes are billed excess amounts and the students are forced to live in substandard housing. Often we are told to charge eight hours of labor and get it done in two hours or less. The repairmen deny that they are responsible for such action. As Mike, a colleague, explained: "Well, you know how it is. The boss says what he wants us to do, and tells us how long it should take us. I know he rode your ass a lot because you took too long to finish a job. We are not given enough time to do the work the way it should be done. But it's not our problem. All we're trying to do is just get by. Besides, it doesn't really matter because the people living there will tear it up again anyway." From my first day on the job I was introduced to the notion of screwing the customer. We are expected to "stick it to the consumer," no matter how we feel about it. If we don't we will be let go.

My boss holds two positions. Officially he is the property manager. He is responsible for renting out apartments in the frat houses and for their maintenance. But he is also in "sales" where he may "bid on a job," making an estimate for materials and labor costs, or he may "go by the job" which means he tells a homeowner how many hours he feels it will take to get the job done and bill them later. In either position there is ample opportunity for corruption. Strange things are done to make up for hours, repairs and ripping of clients. Our company has several divisions. The apartment management company has 15 separate accounts on the books, each having a record of its monthly expenditures. Each account is required to keep track of money. When a housing unit is in need of repair, a check is written for the materials purchased and the amount of time spent on the job is turned in daily. Money from the "home repair account" is kept separately and is put into the other accounts as discrepancies appear. We employ a secretary who works one weekend a month to "straighten out the accounts." This practice clearly violates legal accounting practices. But as one of the repairmen explained: "I am not the boss. I can't do anything about how he runs his business. Like I say, it's really not my problem. I would probably do the same thing if I were the boss."

Repairmen engage in several deviant activities from taking home damaged items, repairing them and charging the homeowner for new replacements, to time theft. Often old work orders are kept around and we are told to make repairs that had been made months in advance. We are told to change our times around to make it look acceptable to homeowners. The boss will typically have ten jobs going on simultaneously to make up hours on different jobs. As Mike says: "It's like when we are told to make repairs that have already been done. Maybe he just forgets. Sometimes he just wants us to kill time. Sometimes he just doesn't have anything for us to do. Hell, I don't mind if he sends us somewhere to do nothing for an hour or two. He keeps me and Tom around and hires and fires other people several times a year. We both know that the company is a scam. It's a big joke (laughing). I don't know how he has kept himself in business all these years."

The games that are played are kind of amusing. The boss makes us angry, so we take it out on those we are making repairs for, which is what the boss wants anyway. We are all capable of doing quality work but are not allowed to. The customer gets angry with us because of the poor quality work we do, but we are told to do it that way.

One of the main reasons the employees felt that our deviant activities take place is because of the company and especially our boss. As one repairman, Mike, said: "He's such a dickhead. He couldn't find his ass with both hands. Remember how we used to make fun of him. He's such an asshole. Here we are, college students, and he treats us like two-year-olds, like we don't know how to use a paintbrush." Mike said that the stuff we did was really a "way of getting even with him. After all, he is making a lot of money off of us, and as far as I'm concerned, doesn't do a thing to earn it. The money we get also helps out."

We get back at the boss by writing in extra hours on our time sheets and saying that we did not take lunch, when we did, so we get a little extra for nothing and the satisfaction of "having screwed the boss." Some of this time we call "windshield time," which means riding around campus looking at the pretty girls, and sometimes we claim to have worked till 6:30 PM when we only worked till 5:15 PM.

The repairmen also pick up various extra perks on the job such as drinking the customer's beer and food. Also when there are materials that are left over from a job, such as nails, plumbing supplies, boards, and other items, these would be taken home for personal use. Again the repairmen found ample justification for this action: "If someone has a case of beer in the refrigerator, I don't suppose they'd miss one. Most of the time they offer me a beer, and if they're not home, I don't see what difference it makes. What they don't know won't hurt them. As far as left-over materials when the job is done, we don't have any place for storage, so we would have to throw stuff away if we didn't take it home. Besides, everyone does it anyway."

Another problem concerns the way we are paid, which is "under the table" with no taxes taken out. Mike said that he didn't mind that because of being only a part-timer: "If taxes were taken out of my check I would make next to nothing. Besides, this is a decision the boss made. He is the one who is responsible. It is none of my business how he does things." This system allows some people the possibility of welfare fraud. They draw unemployment and get a paycheck. Mike justified this saying that, "If a person can get away with it, I see nothing wrong with it. The government screws us all the time so why not? Besides, the guy has a wife and kids."

Chapter 5
Sporting Scams

Ideally, college sports are for students to not only develop physical skills but to learn moral and ethical values, and to learn how to "play the game" without cheating. However, these next three accounts expose a lot more going on in college athletics than playing by the rules. These accounts deal with the cheating that goes on at various levels within college athletics from performance-enhancing drugs to rule violations by coaches.

In the papers by Jay and Winston, steroids are sold to enable student athletes to push themselves beyond the limits set by their physique. For non-competitive weight lifters, such as Jay and his friends, the motive is for a superior physical appearance which will make them feel invincible and the avoidance of being seen by others as weak and puny. Yet use of steroids is seen by others as deviant (not to mention illegal), because it is conceived as cheating. However, its use also brings excitement that can't be achieved without the drug.

Winston examines a range of performance-enhancing drugs used by college football players including steroids, creatine, stimulants and painkillers. He found that these drugs were not only taken so that the athletes gained an edge over the competition, but also to meet the demands of those pressuring the athletes for winning performances, including coaches and parents. Surprisingly, non-using team players provided a protective shield of conspiratorial silence for their using colleagues. They condemned them only if publicity through being caught brought condemnation on the team, but otherwise saw drug use as an individual decision that enhanced the overall team performance.

Ed Bluetowski tells the story about the corruption that occurs off the baseball diamond. Players teach the freshman how to bend the rules on the first day they arrive on campus. One of the most exciting deviant acts is getting to meet your new teammates, not by playing a game of catch, but by getting drunk at the local campus bar. First of all, most of the players are under the legal drinking age, but more importantly, there is a team rule of no drinking during the season. So from the first day of practice, the players have already broken the rules. These players are not just sipping beer. They are buying by the pitcher and slamming down shots. The older players put a lot of pressure on freshmen to drink and the freshmen don't want them to think they're not cool, so they go along. In addition they are taught to cheat on their girlfriends and on their coach. The coach supports the cheating as a form of informal reward for good players, but will punish the inferior players for the very same behavior.

Nor are college athletes immune from more run of the mill scams. Every fall, one of the duties that baseball players must perform is to help park the cars at the football games. This is seen by the players as a nuisance since they have to get up early in the morning to work and don't get paid for it. In order to "get even," the players steal money from the college. They do this by taking the cash from the fans and parking their cars but the players don't turn in all of the money at the end of the day.

These accounts display neutralization techniques, such as the accounts from Ed's baseball team, "The university won't miss the money," and the steroid users in Jay's paper who believe that no one is getting hurt (denial of injury). Jay's colleagues also demonstrate a personal investment: "I want the older players to like me" (appeal to higher loyalties) and use the disclaimer that "there are worse criminals then them," which shows the neutralization of relative acceptability at work. But there were also other ways of freeing oneself from the shackles of law or morality. Steroid use was felt by Jay and his friends to be cheating not because of possible side effects, but because others can't afford its high price. For Winston's football players, drug use was seen as helping the team or a matter of personal morality (examples of an appeal to higher loyalties).

These stories also highlight how status can stem from having something special. In Jay's account, students wanted to have an extraordinary physique that would make them stand out from others. In Ed's account, being a varsity baseball player gives a status, meaning that girls come to you. This need or desire to differentiate oneself from others may tell us much about the social environment that stereotypes people as the same, in this case as students, rather than recognizing their individuality as people.

Athletes on Steroids
by Jay Michaels

Curt and Tommy told me that a buyer was coming that night and I was to be there to witness the sale. They were selling $100 of steroids to him for $175. The guy was a fellow employee of Tommy's who worked in a local health club. Tommy had worked with the buyer but did not know much about him or who his friends were. This was a major concern of theirs because there is always the slim possibility that any potential buyer, who is not known, is a law enforcement official. For this reason they usually only sell to friends or referrals. Because of this there were some intense feelings in the air before the buyer arrived and my friends were somewhat cautious at first. After the buyer entered the room Tommy jokingly asked, "You ain't wearing no wire are you?" The buyer simply shook Tommy's hand and that seemed to be enough to ease the tension. I was introduced to him and treated as part of the crowd.

After a little small talk, the buy took place. Curt placed 100 cc of Equapoise, 200 tablets of Dianbol, and 4 cc of Decdurabolin on the table. This was followed by the placement of $175 by the buyer. The transaction completed, we all began casual conversation. Then the buyer showed us a red price list for a range of steroids, along with other information such as recommendations for the proper mixing of two or more drugs to produce the best results. The price list was two years old and was produced by a now defunct manufacturer of steroids in California. The buyer told us that it was printed on red paper so that "it could not be censored or photocopied." Manufacturers did not want steroid price lists circulating through too many hands for fear that law enforcement officials might obtain copies.

Athletes are introduced to steroids by friends and health club managers. These people convince them that the drugs are effective. All of us in the group are weight lifters. There is an enormous abundance of steroids in the weight lifting setting and they can be obtained very easily in any health club or gym. The perception among the group attending our serious gym is that at least 90% of the members use steroids. They also feel that in the majority of health clubs someone who is employed on the staff is a seller of steroids. Health club employees are around the gym scene everyday and people are always asking them where they can get steroids. This is an easy way for an employee to earn extra money with very little effort. Money is the only motive for selling steroids.

Steroids may come into the hands of health club dealers from a variety of sources. Curt, who claims that he is "number 3 man on the totem pole in the area," makes most of his sales to distributors in the local gyms. He says that most of the steroids manufactured in this country come to us from health professionals such as doctors and pharmacists. Steroids provide an outside profit of tax-free money to supplement their professional salaries. Distributing steroids through the underground economy to friends who are health club managers and then to weight lifters is a very simple procedure. Because they have legal access to drugs for medical purposes, and since there is minimal enforcement of the laws concerning the drug, there is little fear of being caught, provided some caution is used.

Another major source of steroids is smuggling. As with other kinds of smuggling, fantastic stories are part of the knowledge that one picks up as a user. Tommy has heard of people hollowing out surfboards and placing steroids in the cavity and then carrying them across the Mexico/U.S. border. He also tells of them being smuggled in the hubcaps of cars and by way of secret compartments on vehicles. Steroid carriers are able to pass through customs and drug enforcement agencies simply because these agencies are not specifically searching for steroids but for narcotics. Tommy felt that the crackdown on narcotics acts as a "smoke screen" for steroids trafficking.

The main reason athletes use steroids is to achieve certain goals which are felt to be unobtainable without using them. Tommy and Dave are non-competitive weight lifters and their reasons for using steroids center around the idea of being recognized by others as being big and strong so that no one would ever degrade them for being small or "weak looking." These two seemed to have psychological barriers limiting their physical potential which could be broken by the use of drugs. Curt, the only competitive weight lifter in the group, felt that he needed to accomplish goals of size and strength in the shortest possible time and that steroids could help him do this. His ultimate goal is to win as many contests as he can now because, once settled into a career, competition will become relatively unimportant to him. The members agreed that using steroids gave self-respect through accomplishing the goals of winning and sculpturing a superb physique, which was a rare phenomenon in today's society.

Along with the positive effects of steroid use, which are mainly increases in size and strength, there are also some negative effects. These include acne; water retention; mood changes, such as being irritable, restless and aggressive; shrinking of the testes; and sexual aggression. But these changes did not deter the use of steroids because of the overwhelming positive nature of their effects.

Not only did the drastic changes in size and strength appeal to members of the group but the sense of competition was also a major influence. All three members felt that steroids gave them an edge or an advantage over other weight lifters and that using these drugs was the only way to maintain this edge. As Curt said, "The only way to beat the best is to do what the best are doing." This is implying that the best weight lifters are using steroids to become the best and that, "winning appeals to everyone."

Social reaction to steroid use is generally negative. Most people feel that the use of steroids is an artificial way to improve one's body and that athletes who use steroids are cheating because they are not using the ethic of hard work to achieve their goals. The participants do not seem to care what society feels. In the eyes of the steroid user, people react negatively because of jealousy and envy. Curt says, "People become jealous when they see the results I have produced so they degrade me to make their own image look good." He feels that some people want to obtain a good physique, but are afraid to take the step of using steroids to assist them. People are only justifying their own standards by negating his positive accomplishment with their put-downs.

There are no problems coping with the negative reaction of society because the steroid user does not stigmatize himself. In fact, those who use steroids do not see themselves as drug takers in the way that narcotics users are seen as drug addicts. They feel that unlike narcotics, steroids are not detrimental to society even though both are illegal. Steroids produce an overall positive effect on the body whereas narcotics produce a negative effect on the mind and body. For Tommy, "Steroids build up the body not break it down." And although people may not approve of steroid use, it is not as stigmatized as "drug use" by society. This is reflected in the fact that there is very little enforcement of steroid trafficking whereas there is a great deal of enforcement of narcotics trafficking.

Athletes' Little Helpers
by Winston Clark

In spite of society's laws, norms of honest sportsmanship, university athletics department and NCAA rules, which, if broken, can result in suspension or losing a year of eligibility, some college athletes do use performance-enhancing drugs, especially stimulants, steroids, creatine and pain killers. Stimulants like caffeine, in pills or in high caffeine drinks, or other uppers, are used to give an athlete extra energy, especially just before a game; but they are also used to suppress appetite, to keep weight down so as to improve competitiveness. In contrast, anabolic steroids increase muscle size, strength, body weight and speed. Likewise, creatine is a synthetic protein which, when used while lifting weights, can increase the body's weight and strength. Painkillers are used to reduce pain and suffering from injuries, and to allow athletes to continue playing, even when their bodies are not up to it. Some athletes also use them during non-athletic events, just to get through the day.

Estimates vary about the extent of drug use by athletes, from 2% to 4% depending upon the drug in question, with steroid use being down since the 1980s and stimulant and pain killer use up during the 1990s. Research has revealed that the main reasons college athletes use drugs, apart from their physical effects, include: to improve the chances of playing professionally; because of pressure to win by coaches, alumni, students, administration and parents; to level the playing field between themselves and superior athletes; and to restore their former high school standing as top athletes. The studies also reveal a belief among users that they were doing nothing wrong, that no one was being hurt, not even themselves. Interestingly, the research suggests that use is relatively open, even among non-users, and is seen as helping the team as a whole. This may explain in part why non-using team members are not prepared to tell on their cheating peers.

In my own observations in the locker room before and after practice, it was commonplace to find athletes taking pain killers to make it through practice or just be able to make it home after practice. A few even seemed as though they may have been addicted to them because they just kept popping pills to make it through the day. I even witnessed them walking throughout the locker room asking anybody for pain pills. Those who got them from others sometimes took the pills without asking what type they were and how strong each was. I only observed painkillers to be a problem before or after practice or games. I did not observe anyone using painkillers in the weight room.

The use of stimulants in the locker room was also a problem. During the season I have observed a few players taking caffeine pills so they could get through the long practice. Others joked how they used these "pep pills" to make it through the tough daily schedule of being a student-athlete, while some joked the term should really be athlete-student due to the amount of time football consumed in their daily lives.

In the weight room there seemed to be a similar pattern. I openly saw a few members of the team consuming pep pills to get more energy to get through the workout. They shared them as though it was normal practice. I also noted a few players taking creatine. The athletic department had told us earlier in the year that they did not recommend its use and really did not want us using it because there is not a lot of research done on its effects. But in creatine's defense, it can legally be obtained at any GNC or other sporting stores.

Donald, a football player who I interviewed, admitted to taking painkillers and creatine. He said he had been taking them since he began his college career: "You do what it takes to get by." He said he had never been caught or punished for using these substances. He justified his use by saying, "It's a painful game. Without the pain pills I wouldn't be able to play." He said he usually purchased his pain pills and creatine at his local drug store. But he also admitted that he sometimes gets his hands on prescription pain pills on the black market. I asked him if he worried about getting sick or something by getting pills off the black market because they may not really be pain pills like he thought, and could be dangerous. He responded, "I never thought about it." He said he did not get stigmatized for his use of the substances.

Another football player, Neil, had a long history of using stimulants. He said he had been taking them since 10th grade. He did not feel that he was cheating and saw nothing wrong with his behavior. He admitted he started using the stimulants in high school to make weight at wrestling events, since the drugs suppressed his appetite. But he also noticed how much energy they gave him during athletic events: "I just felt like I had enough energy to conquer the world. I did so well I began taking them regularly during games and matches."

He admitted being caught taking the stimulants by an athletic trainer during his freshman year: "I just said it was the first and last time I used them, and he let me go with a warning." But he was never punished for this act. He admitted avoiding the same athletic trainer as much as possible so as to avoid any probing questions from the trainer asking if he was still using the pills. Neil said he never thought about quitting, even though he was caught. "It just made me watch out to see who was watching me."

Anabolic steroids were the substance of choice for Troy. He had been taking these drugs for the past year and 3 months. He began taking them because the coaching staff had changed his position, so he needed to add as much strength and size as possible. "They made me do it. I was too little and weak to play there," commented Troy. "I know it's not right, but hell, I want to play. It's for the love of the game." He engages in a high degree of secrecy to protect himself. He gets his steroids through a body builder he knows in the area. At first, he admitted having a problem finding steroids. He did not want to ask certain people because he did not want to be stigmatized by those who did not use them. He said I was the first person who did not use steroids that he'd discussed this with. He takes injections of the drugs 3-5 times a week. It depends on how hard he's working out and how he eats. "I like to mix it up, so it doesn't appear I got too strong and big too fast. It helps me cover my ass." He knew of the dangers of steroid use, but felt that mixing up the doses would prevent many of the side effects.

Troy said he has never been caught and has yet to be tested for steroid use. He explained that when there were rumors on the team that he used steroids, he would cut back his use. "The only problem I've had was with my back breaking out from time to time." This is a common side effect of steroids. He uses blemish cream to help reduce this problem. But the reaction from those who suspect his steroid use has been mixed: "Most don't care. There has been some alienation from a couple of people who play my position." They view him as a cheater and a poor athlete since he uses the steroids to gain an unfair advantage.

Creatine was the weapon of choice for Earl. He began taking the bodybuilding supplement after he saw the great results that his roommate had with it. "My bench press went up 251 pounds in a month." He also began taking it because he felt his diet was not good enough without it to be his best. He is open about his use of it and is quick to recommend it to others, even though the athletic department is against its use. He did not feel it gave him an unfair advantage: "Everybody in this game is looking for a way to better himself. That's what I did."

Mel was the only person I found to get punished for his drug-using behavior. He was caught using stimulants and paid the price for it: "I started using them to play better, but it turned into an everyday habit." He admitted using uppers daily just for the euphoria it brought him. He was caught during a random team drug test. Since it was his first offense of any kind, the school and coaching staff suspended him for 4 games. He was also put into drug counseling. Missing any of the counseling sessions or failing any subsequent random drug tests would lead to his dismissal from the team and loss of his scholarship. "It made me get my life together and grow up and mature quickly." Mel feels as though he has lost the respect of some of his teammates. "Some of them made jokes behind my back that got back to me." He feels his motives for using the uppers were selfish and altogether a bad decision. Mel got his uppers from a neighbor who dealt drugs, and believes that in time he may have turned to harder drugs had he not received the treatment he needed.

Carlos professes he has a painkiller habit: "I take between 6-10 tablets a day." His teammates call him "old man" because of his use of painkillers. Since this is his last year of playing, he says that he will stop using painkillers as soon as his last game ends. "They allow me to move like a freshman on the field." He also engages in getting illegal prescription drugs whenever possible: "I want the best shit out there." He told me many of his teammates engaged in the same behavior as him. He frequently joked about how upset he and his deviant peers get when no one has any pain pills. "That's when you turn to plan B: go ask the trainers for some aspirin for your headache." Carlos said they frequently use these types of excuses to get pain pills from the athletic trainers. "You've got to know how to work the system or let it work for you." He did not perceive his behavior as deviant: "I'm a grown man! I'll make my own decisions." He knows his pain pill obsession is against team and university rules, but he does not seem to care: "I play by my own rules, not theirs."

"Fitting in" to Varsity Baseball
by Ed Bluetowski

When a player first comes to school and meets the team, there is a lot of doubt in his mind. You are no longer the superstar—the school's only all-state player. Everyone around you has been an all-state player and usually drafted to the professional level. If a player comes to school over-confident, he is quickly reminded that he is just a freshman and that he will be lucky just to make the team. When my cohort of freshmen came in, there were twenty-six recruited players and between one hundred seventy-five to two hundred walk-ons. We had an outstanding recruiting year. Three years later there are only 4 of us left. There is a great need to fit in and go with the punches. No one makes waves, or speaks out, or even considers telling on someone for doing unlawful things.

Bending the rules begins on the first day a new recruit meets the team. One of the biggest scams is parking cars for football games. This work is done by college athletes and can generate quite a bit of side money. The way it works is simple. Each athlete gets an allocation of tickets. Each car entering to park gives him $3. Most people are in a big hurry so if you just happen to forget to give them a ticket, there is $3 in your pocket. The way you figure it is that the team will receive the benefit, you are doing all this work (parking) for nothing and, besides, the school has tons of money. I believe that power and success are measured by the amount of money you have. Everyone is trying to make a buck anyway they can. It seems so innocent and everyone else is doing it too, so why not?

As with most things there is a pecking order for who gets what. The people who get the most money are the senior and junior players. They have been there the longest and if we got caught, they would take most of the blame because the younger players will claim they just follow the lead of the older players. These players could receive, on any given football game, $250-$300. Next in line are the sophomores. They've been around but do not really have that much seniority. They can pull in $150-$200 a night; on a busy night they can easily get $250. The freshmen, who usually run around in the fields parking the cars, only make around fifty bucks, but if there was an older player who Coach did not trust, a freshman may be asked to take money for him. In this case the freshman would have to give the older player half of what he made.

To the freshman this is not a big deal because he would still make more money and the player you gave the money to would like you more.

This might seem like a lot of money, but there are so many cars no one even notices. If a truck would come in with a keg of beer, they are usually let in for free with the understanding that we can drink for free later. When a good-looking girl comes in, she would get in for free, plus get a great spot. These taken-for-granted guidelines are understood by the new recruit within thirty minutes of the first game.

After the game everyone goes to the bar. At the bar the players are let in free. Part of the reason for this is that most of the people that work the door are usually in sports themselves. The older players are usually the ones who buy the drinks for the younger ones. This sounds great, but there is a ton of pressure put on the freshmen to drink a lot. You don't want them to think you're not cool, so you drink.

It starts slowly. Everyone will get a shot and a pitcher of beer. Everyone drinks their shot and a glass of beer, and any time an older player holds up his glass, that is our cue to drink the whole glass. At the end of the pitcher, another shot and pitcher will be waiting. If you are lucky enough to have an older player that likes you, he will come over with an additional shot for you to do. This will go on for two or three pitchers. By this time you are really drunk. Even though you are really drunk you feel lucky because the older players only ask the guys who can drink to go out again.

After the hard drinking is done it is time to pick up the girls. The older players always have girls they know and will usually hook you up with their friends. This is usually hard to get used to because most of the players have girlfriends, but every night you go to the bar they will take a different girl home. To fit in, all the younger players will cheat on their girlfriends too. There is an unwritten code that no one tells anyone of their girlfriends and everyone tries to help the other guy if one of their girlfriends comes into the bar, so she does not see him picking up this other girl. You learn all this the first night, and the next morning you have to be back at the football field to pick up the trash. So by the time your first day is over, you are very hung over, you have cheated on your girlfriend and you have stolen money. You feel like one of the guys, so everything seems fine. You have excuses for everything like "I was drunk," "The university won't miss the money," and "What she does not know will not hurt her" and "I want the older players to like me."

In my junior year the whole system fell when a freshman got caught taking money. In a desperate attempt to keep his scholarship he said that everyone else took money. As a result five people lost their scholarships and everyone else had to run at seven in the morning for 3 weeks. When the wall came falling down I was in Cleveland, playing in the collegiate world series. That night I set a new national record. I came home from the bar at about 3:00 AM and received a call from Coach. He was so mad that he flew me out at 5:00 AM to talk to me. All of the better players were playing with other teams at this time and everyone was flown home so Coach could talk to us. The five people who lost their scholarships were not going to help the team; that is why they were cut. Coach could not cut his good players or we would not be able to win any games. Coach also wanted to keep this from the press because if the NCAA found out, the university would be put on probation. Even after all this I am convinced that next year it will all start again.

In the fall most off us are just like regular students, but what many people do not realize is we practice year round, so even during the off-season we have a lot of pressure on us to perform. In the winter everything changes. The total focus is on baseball and you try to do whatever you can in school. When February comes, I am lucky to make 2 days of classes a week because of practices and games on the road. This puts a lot of pressure on you to get your classwork done without being in class. Perhaps not surprisingly, this results in a lot of cheating and copying. At first you try to pass your classes without cheating but after you fail a couple of tests you will do whatever it takes to get by. In order to stay eligible to play, you have to take certain deviant steps. If you ask anyone on the team what is more important, baseball or school, they will all say baseball. It is really hard to remember that you are here for school when baseball takes on such a major role.

When the season starts all you think about is the game. There is so much pressure put on you to perform that it is difficult to handle. It is hard to make time to see your family, girlfriend or school. Everyone is trying so hard to win a position. There are often conflicts amongst the team. In my first collegiate game I was lucky enough to start. In the 11th inning, I hit a home run to win the game. I was on top of the world. But, in the next game, I missed a sign when I was on second and the coach pulled me out of the game in front of fourteen thousand people. I felt like the biggest asshole in the world. So that night the two older guys I was staying with in a hotel room brought a pint of whiskey, a case of beer, and three girls to the room. The booze and girls are not allowed in our rooms and I was scared to death that Coach would catch us but I felt I had to go along. So we drank everything but 12:00 was bed check and Coach came by our room early. We had the girls hide in the shower and I had to open the door for Coach. I thought I was going to die. I was drunk, there were girls in our room, and Coach was mad at me for missing a sign. So I opened the door, Coach looked at me and says, "You look scared. Don't worry, I am not going to check the shower or anything!" Then he hit me in the stomach and said, "Don't worry about it. Just be ready to play tomorrow." The older guys were laughing because they knew he would not say anything because they were the best players on the team, and he did not want any problems.

The room next to us got in a lot of trouble for drinking, and had to run for 3 hours that night. That showed me that Coach had his own set of rules: the good players can do what they want but if you're not a starter, do not screw up. This also put more pressure on you to be a starter. One night in California, we were playing Cal State. A young pitcher came in to relieve our pitcher, and he did not do too well. That night he said something to Coach. Coach got mad and sent the kid home. I never saw him again after that. That is a really scary feeling knowing that anytime Coach wants to, he can end your career. You must not only abide by the laws of society, you must also abide by Coach's law if you ever plan on succeeding.

As well as the negative pressures of being a part of a team, there are also many positive things. If you talk to one of our players, you will notice how proper they are. This is one of the things that is stressed to us because of our high visibility. We have the chance to travel and see many of the great campuses of the nation. We also have the chance to become professional players, which is each player's goal. I was lucky enough to be drafted professionally out of high school and turned down $85,000 to attend college. I also turned down a pro team this year for $75,000. I decided to stay in school and get my degree and then try to play professional ball.

Chapter 6
Alcohol Antics

Of all the student activities that could be considered deviant, the illegal use of substances is perhaps the most common and the illicit drinking of alcohol by those under the legal drinking age tops the list. In terms of statistical criteria, alcohol use is not deviant, in spite of it being illegal for vast numbers of students who are under the legal drinking age. As the articles in this chapter illustrate, alcohol use occurs in a variety of settings and some of the ways students use alcohol are deviant relative to the norm of student drinking. Moreover, alcohol is illegal, but common use leads to students engaging in other deviant illegal activities, such as using false IDs or buying alcohol for minors.

The account by Bud Bradley on fraternity drinking parties shows how the practice of illegal alcohol use can occur because of the traditions of a particular fraternity, regardless of its legal restriction. Its use is justified on the grounds of loyalty to those traditions and to the membership over the requirements of the university rules and the law (appeal to higher loyalties). In Bud's account and the one by Andy Page on parking lot parties, we see that loyalty to an intimate group can be a strong reason why drinking occurs. For Andy and his student drinking companions the consumption of alcohol actually provides the medium around which intimate groups could meet in a public setting. In this case alcohol changes an otherwise neutral setting to one in which boredom and loneliness can be relieved. Interestingly, alcohol is the catalyst and the subsequent group interaction and trust provides the motive for continued meeting. The group founded on drinking becomes a substitute family for those who, for a variety of reasons, had become isolated from other groups and contacts.

The role of alcohol consumption as a measure of intimate loyalties comes to the fore in the account by Chuck Vincent where it plays a part in college friendships, acts as a bonding agent between those who are far from home and serves as a means of demonstrating independence.

The motives for illicit alcohol consumption are clearly diverse. In addition to structural reasons, Bud documents the individual motives that are behind student drinking behavior. These include the fun that accompanies drinking and the release of tension that it produces, allowing easier conversation and socializing. But less obvious motives are also highlighted. These include the pride from having a reputation of being able to drink more than others or from being able to purchase alcohol for minors. The latter is also seen as a return of favors to a system that provided such services to the purchaser when they were underage. For Andy's friends the use of alcohol actually served as an alternative way of meeting friends and of avoiding having to join circles in which drug use had become the norm.

When accounting for why they engage in drinking and alcohol-related deviant activities, we see that familiar techniques of excuse and justification are used, such as "Everyone else does it" (claim to normality). But some interesting variations are also revealed. We have already mentioned Bud's appeal to the higher loyalties of the fraternity tradition. In addition, he shows how the members make distinctions between occasionally and regularly getting drunk. The latter is less approved. We also see an attempt to condemn the condemners, when minors who ask for alcohol are indulged on the grounds that if they are considered by the government old enough for military service then it is hypocritical to deny them the right to decide to drink. Also questioned is whether there is a significant maturity difference between someone 21 and another aged 17. The issue is that no one is able to sensibly draw the line. Doing so is seen as basically unreasonable. Further, purchasing alcohol for minors is seen as morally responsible since it is part of the education process of learning about responsibilities; how to become a socially responsible drinker. Here we glimpse the claim that deviance can actually be functional to the wider society, also found in Andy's examples of drinking to avoid drug use.

In Chuck's paper, stigmatized labels are used by deviant groups in order to pressure others into deviance. Coping with stigma in these cases focuses upon how students can avoid the condemnatory pressure by peers that comes from not engaging in deviant activity. Whether one can resist the pressure to go drinking depends upon group social acceptance of reasons not to participate. Commitment to schoolwork and girlfriends are shown to be acceptable excuses whereas simply "goofing" results in disapproval. Maintaining a distant relationship with student drinkers frees a fellow student from the obligation to take part. However, exclusion from friendship groups can be the ultimate sanction for those who persistently abstain. Chuck shows that it is not only drinking or not drinking that is subject to such peer pressure, but the amount that is consumed on any one occasion. He discusses informal drinking norms and the use of negative labels that pressure fellow student drinkers to consume higher than normal quantities, with status as the prize.

Each of these articles shows that even when a deviant behavior is commonly practiced, in this case drinking alcohol, the meaning, motives, and consequences can be so different that considering any one type of drinking to be the same as any other drinking behavior can seriously distort any understanding of what is actually going on.

Fraternity Drinking
by Bud Bradley

Fraternities break the laws regarding alcohol every time they have a party. For example, each time we have a party we ostensibly follow the school rules by registering it with the university and with A.B.C. (Alcoholic Beverage Control Board) and by applying for an A.B.C. license. By doing this we follow the rules and the laws of the school and state. We then break the rules by admitting underage brothers and pledges with girlfriends and other friends without checking their IDs. I've allowed minors to use my ID to get into parties and bars, and to buy beer at the Seven Eleven and other stores. My behavior this semester has been no different from any other, except for the fact that I'm now 21 and legally allowed to drink. Whenever the fraternity has a party requiring members to bring a bottle of liquor, I buy the bottles for anyone in the fraternity who is not old enough.

The fraternity has different kinds of closed parties, which are those restricted to brothers, pledges and invited guests. For example, a "room jigger" party is where each room of the house has a different drink. At our

Halloween party each brother and pledge brings a bottle of liquor and pours it into a garbage can filled with mixers and it is drunk as a punch. Some of our parties are held with a sorority. Each of these parties is a tradition within the fraternity, dating back to our chapter's founding.

When the fraternity has closed parties we do not even register them with the university or with A.B.C. By ignoring these procedures we break both the state laws and the university regulations. But we must do it that way. If we were to try to register a closed party the university would not approve it. We would probably have the party anyway because these parties are a tradition within our fraternity. Not to have them would be worse than the trouble we would get into for having them. But the university would alert the A.B.C. and they would be over here arresting people.

When a fraternity gets caught, everybody on campus finds out very quickly because the university goes directly to that fraternity's national headquarters and that is the end of their fraternity on this campus.

We also break the rules by lying about the number of kegs on our license applications, usually halving it. This is a standard procedure of all fraternities. If we did not fudge the application, the party would not be approved and the guys would be demanding a refund on their dues.

Larry, Pete and Billy are members of our fraternity. Larry had not been much of a drinker before he joined. He said that he drinks at the parties because it "opens me up, socially." He drinks because liquor is all that is served and everyone else drinks. He is a quiet individual who enjoys having drinks at a function. He said, "Getting drunk is the best way to blow off steam at the end of a week." By getting drunk at the house he doesn't have to worry about driving home because he can always sleep at the house. He said that the house is a much friendlier atmosphere to get drunk in because you know everyone there, unlike going out to a bar.

Similarly, Pete enjoys drinking because it helps him unwind and allows him to "get happy." He feels that getting drunk allows him to be more at ease socially. He says that drinking and partying are what first attracted him to the fraternity, which has a reputation for having the best parties, and he liked the brothers. Pete takes great pride in the fact that he can drink more alcohol than most people. He gets drunk at the house so that he can get his dues worth. According to him, when he drinks he has more fun than he does when sober, and does things that he would not normally do at a party.

Billy said that drinking is part of what being in a fraternity is all about. He feels that the fraternity puts a bit too much emphasis on drinking but says that alcohol breaks the ice at social functions. He claims that he is "not pressured into drinking if he does not want to" by other brothers. He drinks when he feels like it, and usually if he's had a tough week. He does not drink just to get drunk, saying that this is the first sign of alcoholism. But when it happens, it happens. He thinks that the fraternity occasionally encourages people to get drunk just for the sake of it, but that is just part of being a brother.

I drink because I enjoy having fun and it helps me to do so. I find that I'm more relaxed when I've "had a few," and this helps conversation, especially when I don't know someone that well. I occasionally get drunk. I think that if someone decides to do it, let him or her suffer the consequences. Most of the times that I've done it, I ended the evening by getting sick, and I've seen enough people get sick doing the same thing to have learned my lesson.

In spite of the law and regulations we all give alcohol to minors. Larry explained, "When I was a minor I was given alcohol by members of the fraternity who were old enough and I am symbolically returning the favor. The risks of being caught are not enough to truly worry about." He remembered how tough it was to be underage and to want a couple of beers: "I don't mind buying the guys some beer because someone did it for me." Larry did not feel any moral problem with breaking the law or university rules because, "Everyone else in every other fraternity in this country is doing the exact same thing. The only time I feel deviant is when I go to a party and do not drink!"

Pete thought that if minors want to drink then he has no right to say no because they are old enough to decide for themselves: "If you are old enough to get your ass shot off for your country then you should be old enough to drink what you want when you want." His philosophy about giving alcohol to minors is that, "As long as they don't tell the cops who they got it from then there is no reason why I shouldn't give it to them." Besides, the risks are almost nonexistent: "If the A.B.C. busts one of our parties, the president of the fraternity is going to be the one who goes to jail first, not me." Pete claims that those of us who are old enough are practically required to get alcohol for the minors in the fraternity: "The guys before us broke the law for us, so we should do it for the new guys. We are all here to have a good time, so why should we feel bad or different about allowing the guys who are younger than us to drink?"

Billy's attitude about giving alcohol to minors is that, "College is the time to learn about all kinds of responsibilities, including drinking responsibility." He says that he will not give drinks to anyone who appears to be intoxicated, nor will he deprive anyone of having a good time, "no matter how he intends to have it." Billy says that he doesn't think it is deviant to break the law like this because he did it when he was younger. But he says that so far the fraternity has been lucky in having had no trouble with the law or the university: "Sooner or later we are going to get caught and then there will be hell to pay."

Personally I will only buy booze for people that I trust, whom I feel will act somewhat responsibly with it. I feel that college is a time to learn how to handle alcohol. I serve the minors at our parties only if they want to drink. I never force anyone to do something that they do not want to do. When a minor joins our fraternity or comes to one of our parties, they know that alcohol is going to be served and that they should be man enough to face their own responsibilities and limitations. This doesn't mean, however, that I don't think that every once in a while they can't just tie a huge bag on. That is part of the learning process of alcohol, although an unpleasant part. I don't feel that helping them is socially deviant or morally wrong. It was done for me when I was younger; the younger ones learn to count on the older ones. I feel that I'm no different from any other fraternity brother in the United States of America in giving alcohol to minors. I have no reason to feel guilty for breaking a law that I feel is unreasonable. Who should be allowed to say that just because a person is 21 years old he is more responsible than someone who is 17 or 18 years old? By that age you are old enough to decide what is the best for you. That is also part of growing up.

The recent wave of hysteria about drunk driving has helped to make the behavior of fraternities illegal. Groups such as Mothers Against Drunk Driving and Students Against Drunk Driving have made the public more aware of drunk drivers, especially teens and young adults who have been caught. These groups have put pressure on politicians to pass tougher laws regulating drinking and to raise the drinking ages, making most college freshmen legally unable to drink. These are the same young people who join fraternities, making the fraternities serve alcohol to people who, two or three years ago, would have been legally able to drink. By submitting to the pressure of groups like M.A.D.D. and S.A.D.D., the politicians have turned the fraternities into lawbreakers. In the eyes of such groups, the law and the university, this makes us deviant.

We, however, choose to think of ourselves as not being deviant. We are not the first group to give alcohol to minors, nor will we be the last. One fraternity handbook says that, "In the 1920s some fraternity members were drinking bathtub gin." This was during Prohibition when alcohol consumption was illegal for everyone. So why should we feel deviant about giving alcohol to fraternity members today?

Pressure to Drink
by Chuck Vincent

It is a common understanding that college kids drink because of peer pressure. What causes us to do this and how effective is it? What are the circumstances in which it is more rather than less effective? What about those who do not succumb to this pressure? How do they feel about it and how do they resist it?

When I experimented with role playing and peer pressure in relation to drinking behavior among my college friends, I found that peer pressure seemed to be proportional to school priorities. If someone had important schoolwork to do then I found that peer pressure just did not seem to work. However, it usually worked when the person was just "goofing." When I shook off the efforts of my friends to get out they said, "Some friend you are," and that I was weak and then they waited to see if I would fold. But I never experienced any long-lasting stigma when I stayed at home and my friends went out. I could see their disapproval and condemnation and did not like it but I was also able to dish it out. I noticed that staying in on a Friday night and "catching shit" was quickly forgotten on Saturday night when I went out and drank beers with my friends. However, I was made to feel badly for what I had "missed" the night before. It became evident to me that it was only when one does not go out drinking several times in a row that a person will receive the label "pussy."

Once one of us has been out of the group for a while we do not get back in easily. This seems to be due to the fact that our efforts to get a person to party are rejected and this is taken personally. We feel that the person does not like us anymore.

I also realized that my friends and I often gave way to peer pressure, in spite of our claims that it was not really very influential. I think that denying its effectiveness allowed us to feel that we had more control and independence.

I found that one of the biggest areas where peer pressure operates successfully is in how much we drink. For example, one night I was planning to have only one or two beers because I was running a race the next day. I ended up "slamming" because everyone else was doing it and they were "giving it to me." When certain drinking norms are enforced it is not easy to resist them. For instance, it is not acceptable to fall behind in drinking. If you do so comments are made like: "Come on, man, you are two shots behind. You've got some catching up to do." At this point everyone gets behind the "up man," and the "behind man" has to slam the two shots in order to stay even. If he does not catch up the person is reminded that he is a "lightweight."

In contrast to this behavior, I found that there were ways in which peer pressure could be resisted. Ken was my roommate for all of last year and although my other friends and I used to pressure him to go out with us, he would always resist. I, however, (like some of my other friends) would easily succumb to the suggestion of going to have a shot and a beer even when I did not have the time to go. Ken seemed immune to this. He said that, "The first time you asked me I appreciated it because I felt wanted, but after the thirtieth time I just got pissed off." He said the pressure didn't bother him because he had already made his mind up and it could not be changed. He claimed that his fraternity brothers understood that schoolwork is top priority and they did not criticize him for never going to parties or participating in other fraternity activities. Part of the reason for Ken's resistance to the pressure of his peers was that he perceived himself as independent. He said that he had a negative attitude about school and about this area of the country, and that he "doesn't find partying relaxing."

It seems that maintaining a distant relationship with people enables a person to better resist their requests. In contrast to my relationship with Ken, the one that I have with Chris is more intimate. While it does not matter much if Ken does not want to go out, when one of your closest friends does not want to go out, it calls for even more pressure because it is like being personally rejected.

However, there are legitimate excuses, even among friends. These are accepted as good reasons for not going out and can be used to relieve the pressure to participate in drinking. One of these is having a girlfriend. Chris felt that the pressure placed on him to go out with the guys is much less effective because he has a girlfriend. He feels justified in not always going out with his friends because he has to make equal time with his girlfriend in order to get what he calls a "good mix." He says it is easier to swallow the pressure from guys because they are much quicker to "forgive him" for going out with his girlfriend, while the effects of pressure by his girlfriend are much more long-lasting. He feels that pressure from the opposite sex is more powerful and they can carry the "grudge" much further than would his friends. Chris says he feels more likely to give in to pressure when he is just sitting around doing nothing than when he has to do something particular, like study for a test. Chris basically feels that friends are very important in college and this importance can be used to pressure you into doing things that you might not otherwise do. It was such pressure that made him drink even though he did not plan to do so. He had to "maintain a reputation." Publicly he was strongly against cocaine so his friends didn't pressure him but they could easily get him to go drinking beer or Jim Beam.

Gus, my roommate for the past two years, says he, too, bends under pressure, but he will not buckle if it means going outside his limits. He feels he knows his drinking limit and he will stop once he has had enough, regardless of how far his friends push him. Gus says he feels bad knowing that his friends are out but that sometimes the importance of schoolwork takes precedence. He says that friends are a big part of his life so they influence him to an extent but they know when to stop. They do not put too much pressure on him because they know that "Gus knows what's best for Gus."

In short, I feel that drinking is a big part of college friendships. It is a bond between those of us who are away from home and an occasion where, now that we are all seniors, we can have a reason to go out together. It is also a way of demonstrating our independence from our parents. Peer pressure seems to vary in its effectiveness depending upon the strength of friendships; the importance of other ties, such as those with school and girlfriends; and an individual's own need to be independent or to be liked. No long-term side effects seem to occur to those of us who stay away from drinking once in a while. But those who did not party at all seemed to be viewed negatively.

Parking Lot Parties
by Andy Page

The primary members of this group first met at an illicit outdoor party which had taken place in a parking lot of a rural community college. Most of those at the social gathering knew each other. The particular social group that I was involved with did not emerge overnight. As with most friendships, it takes a certain amount of time for each person to evaluate the others to see if the friendship is worth pursuing.

The members of this group had a lot in common. They were all of roughly the same socioeconomic class, all college students, all had some common friend or acquaintance, all consumed alcohol regularly and all normally consumed alcohol in public places such as parking lots.

After two weeks, which involved three or four chance meetings, the group began to meet regularly on average twice a week, usually Tuesdays and Thursdays. They would get together in the same parking lot in which they had originally met. The primary members of the group were two males and two females between the ages of 19 and 25. All lived within thirty miles of the party location which in rural areas is not far to travel to such an activity.

Even though the group was meeting on a regular basis they still did not know each other very well. It was not until inhibitions were lowered, usually a result of drinking beer, that members began to become close friends. They began by simply lying in the sun, drinking beer, telling jokes and relating each other's past experiences. As time went on conversations of past experiences became more and more personal. An unbelievable level of trust in each other developed. As this trust developed, so did the length of time devoted to the group and the amount of beer consumed. The time spent together lengthened from five to ten hours per meeting, and Friday and Saturday nights were added to the meeting days. For three months the relationships between the primary members of the group were very close. During this whole time there was no sexual contact or dating within the group; only recently have two of the members begun an intimate relationship.

As time went on it became apparent that this group served certain functions for its members. A central function was that of relieving boredom and loneliness. As one of the girls in the group said, "It gives me something to do and a place to go where I can be myself." She related how she had never been asked out on a date with anyone she wanted to go on a date with and that most of her friends were married or dating steadily. The other female in the group had stopped associating with most of her old friends because they were, "too wild and crazy" for her to relate to any more. It seems that most of her old friends had gotten heavily into drugs. She herself had been addicted to amphetamines and was afraid of being tempted to use the drugs again. The male in the group had also lost most of his friends through marriage and said that we were all he had left.

Another function served by the group was mutual support. It offered an outlet for members to express their feelings, thus relieving tensions and frustrations in their life. For example, one of the female members had family difficulties. She had a stepmother whom she could not stand. Most of her life she had been raised by her grandmother. In the past couple of years she has been living with her father and his much younger wife. Like all the core members in the group she did not care to spend much of her time at home or around her family. In a sense the group had become her second family.

The group had a strong identity such that our individual views of those people outside the group became the views of the group as a whole. Most of these were expressed as dislikes about certain other people. It was seldom that a member of the group would defend an outsider and as a result the list of outsiders that were disliked became larger. It also seemed like the list of outsiders disliking the group became larger. For a time the group isolated itself more by leaving the parking lot and going off to a secluded place called "The Loop" which was an old lumber road located off a secondary road. This move was made not only to get away from other people in general, but also to get away from increased state police patrols in the college parking lot. The rumor, which came from trusted faculty at the college, was that the increase in state policing had been caused by complaints from college officials about alcohol consumption and parties in the college parking lot. Twice the group was warned and threatened with arrest by the state police. Not wanting to get into trouble the group began taking precautions to avoid confrontations with the law.

For the first three months the group remained stable, but shortly after that the time that its members spent together, as a whole, grew less. This was in part because its members went back to school and college work required a change in each member's schedule, which up until now had run concurrently. Another factor was the development of an intimate relationship between two of the group members, which resulted in these members cutting early from the group. It is almost as though these members felt uncomfortable being around, especially when there was a third member present. In spite of this, the group still meets more or less regularly and each member still shares a close bond.

Clearly our group demonstrates that those who drink in public places are not necessarily only skid row alcoholics. The meeting of our group in a parking lot constituted a social group that supplied intimate relationships lacking elsewhere in each of our lives. Drinking alcohol was the medium through which we met and sustained these relationships.

Chapter 7
Marijuana Merriment

Smoking marijuana is one of the more common drug activities on university campuses. It is also one of the most social. The "high" or "buzz" experienced is considerably enhanced by being shared with others. As the student accounts in this chapter demonstrate, its use is learned in a group setting, its effects are learned from others, it is consumed by sharing either a pipe or cigarette, and it is enjoyed through celebrating its effects with fellow smokers.

Paul Jones explains how learning from others how to smoke the drug and enjoy its effects involves a process of mimicking friends and receiving approval for correct responses. Stan Vaughn points out that this initial experience is often something undergone at 15 with high school friends. Initial experiences are not universal according to Paul's respondents, who explain that it may involve an unpleasant paranoia and fear of losing control before one learns to experience a pleasurable high.

Stan's paper shows that the motives of teenage users may have more to do with status acquisition than the drug's mind-altering effects. Paul and Lana Wilson make it clear that while a high is experienced by many smokers, individual motives for using the drug vary from it being a distraction from problems and a relief of boredom or a way of becoming mellow, to being a source of a thrill without side effects. Paul points out the similarity between the motives for marijuana smoking and under-age drinking, in that both allow the person to create excitement from the very fact of the illegality of the behavior and the sense of "beating the system." But one of Lana's associates says that if social life were more satisfying, it would be unnecessary to use the drug at all.

All three accounts reveal a technique of justification in which the drug is claimed to be less harmful and more pleasurable than the more socially acceptable consumption of alcohol or the less socially acceptable consumption of hard drugs (claim of relative acceptability). Alcohol is seen as more expensive, more physically damaging to the consumer and more hazardous to others in society. Even when officially arrested for marijuana smoking, the contrast between this behavior and that of worse offenses is used to exonerate those who might otherwise feel morally condemned. One of Lana's fellow students draws on the metaphor of the ledger, suggesting that all the good things he does with his body to promote health must be weighed against his marijuana smoking, and when that is accounted for he comes out on the healthy side. Another draws on the relative inaction by social control agents, such as the police, to suggest that it is actually acceptable to officialdom, in spite of being illegal. A similar point is made by Stan who claims that dangers of being caught are a myth, that police, parents and even state legislators have accepted marijuana as not particularly serious. Indeed, his denial of the seriousness of marijuana smoking is yet another variation of the neutralization technique of denial of injury, which might best be called the denial of importance.

That marijuana is illegal, however, leads to various attempts to maintain the drug's secrecy. Paul's student smokers engage in elaborate ritualized precautions against being caught and for them these practices become part of the fun of using the drug. The secrecy also enables these occasional smokers to avoid the socially stigmatizing label of "dope addict" that accrues to regular users. In contrast, Stan's friends neither care nor cover up their smoking, and claim that their occasional use never attracts the label "pothead."

Overall these papers suggest that since the late 1980s smoking pot has become a relative non-issue. Indeed, the reality is that while it is still deviant from the wider population's practices, and a conviction of having used it will deny a person a position as a Supreme Court judge, it will not bar one from consideration for a job with the Secret Service or the FBI, or for that matter, from becoming President, provided the crucial "experimented" spin is put on usage. In short, concern about marijuana smoking has been supplanted by concerns for other deviant activities. Indeed, there is a sense that pot smoking has lost some of its charm and status as a recreational deviant activity, and in the 1990s it even became legal for medical use in California, while cigarette smoking became increasingly criminalized nationwide. And all this should tell us something of the historical relativity of moral standards and the necessity of placing any consideration of deviance in the wider socio-historical context.

The Bong and the Weed
by Lana Wilson

The TV is on but nobody is watching it. The main attraction is a foot-high purple plastic tube with a bowl on its side. This is a bong. Everyone's attention is focused on Morris who is putting marijuana into the bowl. The marijuana is lit and long airy inhalations are made on the bong. They all wait their turn to smoke the weed. This passing around of the bong goes on for about half an hour until everyone is high. Everyone seems more relaxed now. They sit further back on their chairs and their attention leaves the bong and the baggy filled with weed. They talk about many different things, about things not pertaining to the drug: school, weight lifting, girls, what they did last weekend and what they will do this weekend. But they also talk about things that do pertain to the drug: how much it costs, who it was obtained from, what kind it is, and how good it is. Every now and then one or the other will state how high they are. They don't linger on the subject. They bring it up just long enough so that everyone else knows that they are high.

Wilber, Morris and Leroy were all introduced to smoking pot by family or friends. Wilber said, "I don't know anybody who didn't start smoking pot because of peer pressure." They each learned how to smoke pot by watching someone else use the drug. Although many people don't get high the first time they smoke it, Leroy felt that his state of mind had definitely changed and Wilber felt that he was not in total control the first time that he tried it. They both felt that a person who smokes pot will just know the experience when they feel it, but these guys have been smoking for ten years and may have forgotten what it was really like when they first began.

Leroy enjoys smoking because it makes things more thrilling, but Wilber and Morris smoke pot because it has the effect of mellowing them out, taking their minds off their problems. It allows them to withdraw and escape from things; it relieves tension and stops them from worrying. Pot smoking also relieves boredom. Wilber believes college is boring and that smoking pot helps relieve this: "I always seem to find something to do when I'm high. Even smoking takes time." Morris likes it because it is quick to take effect, produces no hangover and makes people smile: "Two bong hits or a couple of hits off a joint and I'm buzzed. It's not like you have to drink a whole case of beer or something. And you don't wake up feeling like shit the next day."

Although smoking pot is considered deviant by the public it is acceptable among these guys because, said Leroy, "Even though it is not the norm of society, enough people do it to make it acceptable," while Morris and Wilber did not care what the public thought about their activities. Indeed, they do not just excuse it, but justify the behavior. For Leroy there is nothing at all wrong with pot smoking and he believes that it should definitely be legalized. Interestingly, Wilber believes that it should remain illegal because if it were freely allowed it would be abused. He believes that "people shouldn't need it if they have a full life." Morris thinks that governments outlaw marijuana because they don't know enough about it and he believes that more research ought to be conducted to see what its effects on the body really are. Here again the comparison was made with alcohol. Wilber argues that if marijuana remains illegal then alcohol should also be illegal because its effects are worse: "There are so many accidents caused by alcohol. I don't know of any accident that has been caused by someone high on pot."

Wilber had been arrested while at high school for drug-related activities. This was the same school that his father had attended and he said that he was embarrassed for letting down his whole family. But when Morris was arrested while smoking pot with his friends, he experienced a sense of injustice and shame. He had been the only one arrested because he was the one holding the joint: "I felt bad when they took me down to the jail but when I compared myself to the people there who kill and rob, it didn't feel that bad." According to Morris this view is given some support by the police themselves. He claimed that the police generally treat pot smoking in different ways from the way they respond to other crimes. "Most don't think that pot smoking is too bad." He said when he had only small quantities most cops just let him go: "The only time they treat it like hard drugs, such as cocaine or heroin, is when massive quantities are involved." Unofficial reaction to marijuana smoking is not much of a problem. Wilber said that there used to be a time when people would stereotype all young people with long hair as pot smokers, but not any more. He doesn't feel that people know he smokes pot and if they do, he doesn't care. Nor does Leroy: "It's part of me and part of my life, so coping with what other people think comes easy." Morris doesn't think that pot smoking should attract negative stereotypes because it is not as bad as other things people do: "It's not as bad as old women who pop pills or drunks." Morris lifts weights and feels that since he takes care of his body and his health, people shouldn't knock him just because he smokes a little weed: "Does the guy who speaks against drugs do anything with his body? I may smoke pot but at least I lift weights and exercise. All I do is smoke pot and I think that is pretty trivial. It's not like I get doped up every day like some do."

Of the three, only Wilber plans to quit sometime in the near future. He feels smoking joints slows him down and he doesn't want smoking pot to hurt his chances in the job market. Morris and Leroy both intend to continue smoking pot. Morris isn't planning to quit in the next few years but he said that in the future when he starts a family he doesn't plan to smoke in front of his children: "I'll probably quit when I start a family but I won't know for sure until that happens." Leroy doesn't think he will ever quit. He says, "My parents always smoked it when I was growing up and I plan to smoke it until I no longer can."

Marijuana Smoking
by Paul Jones

The people in my group of friends that smoke marijuana began as a result of pressure from peers combined with a general curiosity. When their friends started smoking marijuana it became "the thing to do" and it made them wonder what it was like. As one member said, "No one jammed a joint in my mouth and made me smoke it." General curiosity about the drug and repeated offerings of the substance by friends made the decision to try it a lot easier.

It is difficult to establish the initial experiences of marijuana users since years may have elapsed from the time they first began smoking it. The general consensus is that the effect of the drug varies from individual to individual. One member I spoke with said that when he started smoking he was not particularly free because he didn't know how to act or how he was supposed to feel. So he acted the way the other people around him acted and was pleased when they commented approvingly that he smoked like he'd been doing pot for years. Now he smokes the way he wants to and feels that he can enjoy the drug more as a result. Another member said that when he first started with marijuana he felt paranoid. This feeling was caused by uncertainty about the effects of the drug but, with experience, he learned to enjoy the effects more.

Marijuana smoking usually only occurred on weekend nights to avoid interference with schoolwork. It was almost always accompanied by the consumption of alcohol in the context of a small party at one of the guy's apartments. Before smoking actually began many precautions were taken such as closing the windows, dead bolting the door and not permitting strangers to enter after the activities had begun.

At first everyone would play drinking games such as "buzz" or "quarters." At one point during the game, three or four of them would get up from the table and go into one of the back bedrooms. The bedroom door was locked and the group would get stoned. They rolled the marijuana into joints, mixing it with tobacco and using cigarette papers stuck together to form a fat cigarette. This would be passed around the group with each member taking a few puffs in order to get high. When they came back from the bedroom they would continue to drink with the others in the apartment.

The effect of combining alcohol and marijuana is a more intensified high. As one member of our group said, "The main objective is to party as hard as you can for as long as you can." However, the effects of marijuana and alcohol are different. I was told that whereas alcohol made him feel obnoxious, marijuana made him feel "laid back and relaxed. Marijuana gives a more self-contained high." This effect had a tendency to allow the marijuana smokers to stay at home for the rest of the night rather than go out with their friends. But another reason for staying at home is because continued use of the drug over time minimizes its effects. For one member, the effects of marijuana have worn off so much that all he presently gets out of the drug is a tired feeling which often makes him want to go to bed and sleep it off.

Another motivation for marijuana smoking, mentioned by one of our group, was the sense of "getting away with something." He compared smoking marijuana to drinking alcohol when you are underage. It was exciting to smoke this drug because there was a chance of getting caught, and by not getting caught you were beating the system. This may be one reason why this group made such a ritual of the pre-smoking precautions.

A more obvious reason for this secretive behavior was that the members did not want outsiders to know that they smoked marijuana. For one member, this was necessary simply because he did not want to be arrested; but another said that he "did not want people to exaggerate the truth and make him look like a dope addict." All of these members were aware of the stereotype of the "dope fiend" envisioned by people who do not participate. This particular group viewed themselves as full-time college students who only participate in marijuana smoking on weekends as a recreational drug. They do not want to be labelled "potheads" or "burnouts," and be scarred for life as a result.

In short, the basic strategy that this group uses to avoid the stigma associated with their deviant behavior is to conceal it from others. They did this in a number of ways, from locking doors before using the drug to not talking about the behavior to anyone other than trusted friends. It is for this reason that pot is only smoked with trusted friends or alone.

Catching the Buzz
by Stan Vaughn

According to the annual survey of American high school students conducted by the University of Michigan, over the last ten years between 55-60% of senior high school students consistently report having tried marijuana at least once. It seems to be the most popular drug after alcohol and cigarettes. In light of this it is not surprising that three fellow students I interviewed began their use of the drug at high school. They said they began around age fifteen. For one it was his brother who first introduced him to marijuana. For the others it was school friends. As one said, "Everyone wanted to be cool like the upperclassmen in high school."

All agreed that at first it wasn't much. But after trying it a few times they began to catch a real buzz. Now they tend to smoke it on social occasions just like drinking. It has become a kind of social toy with friends. Whenever there is a party, people will bring some along to enable others to socialize and get high. The way they smoke is with a "bong," which is a long cylindrical tube with a pipe attached to it. Inhaling the smoke this way is smoother on your throat and lungs.

My friends prefer bong hits to drinking alcohol for a number of reasons. In the first place, as one said, "It's cheaper than beer and gives you a better buzz. You have to drink six to twelve beers to catch the same buzz you get with one bong hit." It was also pointed out, "There are no side effects from smoking like there are from drinking. You don't have to worry about puking if you smoke too much." Some people think that marijuana is expensive, but again it is not as expensive as alcohol. A "dime bag" which costs $10 can usually be used for a full weekend whereas you could spend $10 in an hour at a bar buying alcohol. Because most of our friends use it, it is very easy to find and it often pays for itself. Sometimes my friends would buy a quarter of a pound and sell it for a profit. That way they wouldn't have to pay for their personal use of it. But this sale of drugs is not a big deal. It only occurs in small quantities. As long as the drug stays in our group they feel relatively safe.

The issue of safety or the dangers of being busted are myths. Being caught and punished for smoking is almost laughable. Most of my friends have been caught but no harsh penalties were inflicted. One of us got busted for possession. It started out by him being pulled over for speeding on the marine base. The police officer saw a bag of marijuana lying on the floor and all that happened was he got banned from the base. As another friend said, "As long as you are only carrying small amounts the cops won't bust you." One said that his dad found his bong in the car one day and all he did was throw it away. All agreed that they frequently smoked in their parents' houses while their parents were home. It seems that both the police and parents have accepted marijuana smoking as not particularly serious. Right now a number of the states have decriminalized possession of small amounts.

No one was bothered that there were some people who thought their activity was deviant. In their minds the only way they got labelled was by the courts. Other people are just not shocked by it. Perhaps the most negative label attached to those who smoke marijuana is "pothead." My friends never earned that label in high school because it is usually reserved for those who were extreme drug users rather than the social users that I spoke with. I don't think labelling is an issue with marijuana. It is just not that important. I think most of them will smoke it whether it is legal or illegal simply because they enjoy getting high.

As the drug of the 1980s, cocaine became synonymous with the new materialism. Just as marijuana and LSD complemented the popular culture of the sixties, producing mind-altering affects that allowed dream, fantasy and reality to merge, so in the eighties cocaine lent itself to the fast fix and high bucks. With a popular culture emphasizing high risk, quick satisfaction, and large material rewards, cocaine became a drug of preference for over and underachievers alike, and it may be the first classless drug outside of alcohol. The style of use varied from powdered cocaine that was snorted or sniffed or injected to "crack" that is smoked. These different forms produced a difference in the criminalization of the drug as "crack," preferred by African-Americans, was penalized ten times more severely than the powder form, preferred by whites. However, as we have already seen, because we take an activity to be significant does not mean that all those who participate in it behave similarly or share the same understanding of what it means or motives for doing it.

The articles that form this chapter point both to similarities and differences in the way students use the drug. From Michele Grant we learn how cocaine use involves exclusive networks of friends and a specialized private language, and yet it also has aspects of use which occur in public settings. She describes how coke is used and how it is dealt to make large profits. Lisa Smart's catalogue of coke characters displays the variety of motives behind the drug's sale and use. Both Lisa and Carol Hodge show how cocaine users can sustain a belief in their invulnerability to harmful physical and social consequences of this form of illegal deviant activity, the reality of which is denied by Kenny Morgan's contribution. Kenny shows us how easily the public and private settings of drug use can be penetrated by control agents, with disastrous consequences for the participants. Each of the papers shows us the range of substance abuse activity from user to dealer.

The students in these accounts got involved in cocaine use through friends at school, at parties or in the privacy of a home. Unlike the pressure that we saw actively encouraging the use of alcohol, cocaine use seems to be more of a voluntary decision in which the use by friends, without apparently dire consequences, is perhaps the main draw. Once involved in a network, students get to know suppliers at their workplaces, typically in bars and restaurants, and may, in turn, eventually become suppliers themselves. Lisa shows that being involved with friends who use cocaine provides numerous occasions where the drug will be offered and, even if initially declined, a subsequent occasion may result in a first try that can lead to subsequent use. Being prepared to try the drug is shown to be facilitated at parties by the use of alcohol which lowers inhibitions against trying anything.

The motives for using cocaine are varied. Initially it may be simply curiosity to see what everyone else sees in the drug, as Carol's account reveals. The first or even subsequent experiences are not always pleasurable and can result in terrifying hallucinations or simply in an unpleasant taste in the mouth and throat, as Michele and Carol's accounts testify. Clearly, for those who experience the drug pleasurably, the high is intense and exhilarating, giving a feeling of energy, a sense of escape or invincibility, resulting in relaxation and even, as Carol says, prestige from belonging to the "in group."

The motives for dealing can be as simple as the case of Kenny's friends who were doing it so they could snort for free; or to help out fellow friends through a reciprocity of favors, as with some of Michele's network; or for the high profits that can be obtained, as Lisa documents. In one of her cases, dealing was being done to earn enough money to be able to start a legitimate business.

The major stigmas associated with the media discussion of cocaine use are met with a variety of responses. Secrecy, private parties and obvious precautions of restricting networks to trusted users and dealers enable participants to avoid the more direct condemnation and consequences of their activity. Michele relates the indifference which her fellow students held for detractors, with one believing that "If you let people get to you you're a bigger fool than they are." For others, the down side of the drug's effects was more of a deterrent than what society thought and, as Lisa shows, for those with cocaine experience, the media anti-drug campaigns seem to be seen as simply sensationalism. Interestingly, the bonding between students and their parents does seem to make a difference, with students not wanting their parents to find out about their involvement for fear they would be hurt by the knowledge.

As in the case of other deviance, cocaine use has its range of rationalizations which free the participants from the moral implications of what they do and enable them to sustain a morally acceptable self-image. Classically, the occasional versus regular use is one such technique, and another is the right of individuals to decide what they want to do with their own lives. For some it is enough that they earn money legitimately rather than through theft or other illicit means, and this seems to exonerate them from culpability. Ironically, the media stereotype which presents drug use as a low-life activity is denied. Instead, taking cocaine is seen as different from other drug use; users claim it does not result in the failure of a person to sustain the rest of their life, either socially or economically. Indeed, even the dealers are able to distance themselves from negative stereotypes by making distinctions between what they do and the practices of other drug dealers who may sell drugs to children; what they do may not be legal but they do not see themselves as bad.

Cocaine: A Guide
by Michele Grant

My connection with cocaine was through my brother and his friends. When I first heard about the drug it was not as cocaine since it was more often referred to as "coke," "snow," "dust," "blow," "snow-caine," "nose candy," and "the ultimate drug." A central connection shared by members of the group is their employment. All of the coke users my brother introduced me to worked in restaurants somewhere in the area. Here they met other people who were involved in the use and/or selling of cocaine.

To obtain the drug it is necessary not only to know the right terms and to frequent the right places, but also to be a member of an accepted group. The people who frequent places where coke is obtained vary from night to night, with only a few who can always be found there. Getting involved in the activity is not so much a matter of what you know but who you know. After you've been accepted as "safe," that is, not a police officer, the friends will lead you to a "contact." Sometimes the contact is a member of the group; many times they are not.

Friendships among members of the group are strong and reciprocal. For example, if the group from Slatters went down to the Bistro they would receive extraordinary services; drinks are poured generously and made with good liquor as opposed to the cheap stuff that is usually used. In return the group would leave a large tip, usually 25% of the bill. This reciprocity of favors occurs wherever the group goes.

My brother's main contact was his friend, Ted, who sold him cocaine that had not been "stepped on" or "cut," which means that it was purer than general street cocaine. At other times we would go to see a new contact, and these are abundant. People who run the front doors of bars checking IDs are usually dealing, but I was advised to avoid new people because of the possible dangers. Others who are around the group are also to be avoided, such as "cocaine cowboys," who are cocaine smugglers, and "coke whores," who are people who beg or borrow cocaine and rely on others for "free rides."

Coke can be administered a number of ways. The most popular way is to string out lines of the drug to be sniffed through a straw, often made of a rolled dollar bill. Another way to do the drug is to use a "coke spoon," on which the drug is carried to the nostrils where it can be sniffed or "snorted." More recently a version called "crack" has become popular since this can be smoked.

The high or "buzz" one gets from coke "takes you up physically and mentally such that you don't want to come down. It is an exhilarating feeling," said one of the group, while for another coke "intensifies your personality." In their pleasurable state of high people are described as "cocainized," "coked out," "coked up," "snowed" or "wired." The experience is not always pleasurable, however. For example, sometimes people experience hallucinations such as "coke bugs," which is the sensation of insects crawling on your skin. Another bad part of taking coke is "crashing" or, as it is also called, the "cocaine blues." This is the depression that follows the high after using cocaine.

Clearly many people use cocaine for the pleasure of being wired. For others in our group it was what that feeling represented. Some speak of a sense of "escaping" from the world and from their troubles by using the drug. They describe how their problems do not seem to matter while they are high.

For those who are into cocaine for the profits that the drug can produce, the simplest and most common system is to "step on" cocaine using Isotal. This means using another chemical to reduce or "cut" the purity of cocaine. A particularly popular formula for doing this is known as "eight ball." This involves mixing 3.5 grams of cocaine bought for $275 with 1 gram of Isotal and dividing the mix into 4½ 1-gram packages to be sold at $100 per gram. The resultant income is $450 which, less the original cost, produces $175 profit or around 64%. (These were 1986 prices.)

Dealing cocaine is not the only profitable activity that some of those who use cocaine are into. The same people who are selling and using cocaine are also involved in other rackets such as smuggling fake Rolex watches into the country and "ripping off people" with over-priced car repairs.

The members of our group are rather dismissive of what other people think about their use or dealing in cocaine. Most of them had not had to confront official reaction to their behavior although one was currently in court for possession of ¼ ounce and two counts of intent to distribute. I was told, "The accepted smart thing to do in such a situation is to make a deal with the police," and, "Dealers commonly make deals in this way to receive more lenient sentences." Some said it didn't matter what society thought, and another said, "To hell with society." One member believed that cocaine users hide behind the drug and "almost eliminate themselves from the opinion of society." But another said: "It's like anything else. If you let people get to you, you're more of a fool than they are." My brother stressed that while he was using cocaine he was not interested in listening to what other people thought. But, at other times, when he was confronted with what society thought, he realized that he "was wrong and wanted to be accepted." He added, "There isn't a day when I don't wake up feeling like scum. But I hold my head up high and try to lead a normal life." Since he quit using cocaine he has never felt better and stated that he's "glad that it's now over."

College Kids as Coke Characters
by Lisa Smart

The following accounts are taken from interviews with three fellow students who were each involved with coke at different levels of seriousness and frequency.

Adele, an occasional user:

> I guess I was about 19 when I started with coke. It was after Brett and I had been dating for about a month. Brett had been using coke for about a year. He never snorted in front of me, but one night I felt like trying it just for the hell of it. Brett had offered it to me a few times before and I'd turned it down. But I thought I'd give it a try to see what the big deal was all about.
>
> Cocaine gives me a lift. I get so tired from school and work that I need something every once in awhile to get me going. I use it more often when I'm tired. My moods don't really control my use of cocaine. Last year when Brett and I broke up I was really depressed but I wasn't using coke. Maybe this was because I couldn't get it or because I wanted to be depressed.
>
> I think it's a good idea that the media focuses on coke. It's good to teach young kids to stay away from it. It really is bad stuff. But as you get older you can make your own decisions. I am old enough to make my own decisions. I don't need everyone and their brother telling me what to do. The government can try to control it, but it's impossible to stop people from using drugs. Right now it is just a passing fad to say "no" to drugs. Next year I bet no one will remember the whole campaign.
>
> I only know a handful of people who use cocaine. I think it is overrated. I don't use it that often, maybe twice a month. It gets expensive. As for my health, I haven't noticed any change. I'm not afraid of dying from cocaine.
>
> I don't think I am low class. I'm not living on the street begging for money. I have never had anyone tell me I'm a scrub bag because I use cocaine. I think that the lower class stereotype of the drug user is a bunch of crap. I don't consider other coke users low class. There are a lot of terrible people in this world, both drug users and non-drug users."

Brett, a regular user:

The first time I used cocaine was when I went away to college. I was eighteen. It was at this huge party. I was real drunk and I saw a couple of my roommates trying it, so I gave it a try too. It was great stuff and it didn't give me a hangover.

I like the high, the energy it gives, and the fact that I don't have to worry about throwing up or having a hangover the next morning. Cocaine helps me get through late nights. It also gets me in a good mood for a party. I don't drink anymore so I need something to get me relaxed.

I think that all the media attention that cocaine has received is just a fad. A couple of famous young people drop dead from cocaine and the whole United States goes crazy. If it had been me that dropped dead last summer and not Len Bias, no one would have even cared. I am sure people drop dead left and right everyday from drugs and no one seems to give a damn about them. I think Nancy Reagan doesn't have anything better to do but to have a little campaign to screw with.

I'm not afraid of the health consequences. Maybe someday I'll have a close call or Adele will. That might make me wise up and really look at what I'm doing. As for my health I think I'm okay.

I'm not saying that the subject is over-reported. There are certainly a lot of people using it. I know lots of people who use it just every once in awhile; then there are people who use it all the time.

The idea that drug users are low class is a bunch of bullshit. Yeah, the ones in the street may be pretty low but I don't consider myself to be low class. First, I'm not addicted to coke. Second, I work for a living. I went to college, got a degree and now work for a very prestigious engineering firm. Third, I pay for my coke with my money, the money I earn from working my butt off. That druggie on the street probably mugged an old lady to get the money for his habit. The dealers who deal to little kids are scum.

I wouldn't want my little sister or your little brother to start using it. Most of my friends who use coke are pretty respectable people. All of them have nice jobs and good families.

Brian, a dealer:

I started using coke at a party. I met Brett there. It was a loud party given by some fraternity. I was pretty hammered. I didn't feel pressured at all. I just tried it like everyone else did. I was so drunk I probably would have tried anything.

To tell the truth I don't use much of it personally. I was more interested in the business side of cocaine. I began to deal cocaine when I was in college. There were several of us dealing. Then I dropped out of school. I got a big day job. What a joke. But my coke dealings are my main source of income. I work on my own. It's amazing. I cleared $50,000 tax-free last year. You could never imagine how easy it is to succeed in this business. My first year back from college was an excellent dealing year. I cleared $100,000. I was so afraid that my parents were going to find the money. I stuffed it in a mattress in an abandoned house. But then my parents were transferred and I stayed behind to live here. I don't have to hide my money now—just from the government!

I snort every once in awhile. I am afraid I will start to like it and snort all my profits up my nose. Money is the main reason I do this. I love it. If it weren't for the financial rewards, I wouldn't be here. It's so nice to be able to have what you want. I can buy gifts for everyone. See these. They are one-carat diamond earrings. Do you know how much they are worth? I'm giving them to my mother for Christmas this year. She always wanted diamond earrings. My family has never had a lot of money. I think it's our turn to be rolling in it.

I guess I also like the business side of it. I like meeting new people when I deal.

The media hype doesn't bother me. My business is booming. That campaign is directed to little kids. I'm only concerned with the big kids. I think the United States is getting paranoid, afraid that drug users are out to destroy the country. Coke users are just a target of the media this time around. It's just a passing thing.

I am a low-class person living in a high-class apartment and driving an expensive car. I think there are some coke dealers that are pretty seedy. There are some bad, very bad people out there in this business. But there are good people too. It depends upon the type of person. I'm just me, Brian. Take me as I am. I don't deal to kids.

Maybe someday I'll quit dealing. I can't see myself doing this ten years from now. I want to start my own legal business. So if and when I start a family, I'll be away from all this. I'll probably leave this town someday to get away from it all. I have never been caught. I've been lucky, very lucky.

My Brother Does Cocaine
by Carol Hodge

I had been over to my brother's house many times when he and his friends were doing cocaine. I had even participated at times so this made these particular discussions relaxed and informal.

My brother, Carl, had his first experience with cocaine when he was seventeen and a junior in high school. One of his friends had some cocaine in his locker at school and asked if he wanted to try it. They did it in the parking lot. Carl had agreed because the guy was a friend and he wanted to see what it was like. He didn't do it again until a year later when the same friend offered him some more. He said he enjoyed the first experience but could not explain why it had taken a year before he did it again.

After this second time the occasions of its use became more frequent. In his senior year he started going to parties on weekends and the people that he hung out with always had cocaine. They would drink and then somebody would set up lines. He said that he enjoyed doing cocaine because it always woke him up at parties and made him feel more lively and full of fun.

There was no negative social reaction within his circle of friends: "No one cared if there was cocaine at a party and most people were glad that there was." Most of his friends approved of the behavior. However, within our family there was some concern. Our mom found out about six months ago that Carl was doing cocaine because my older brother, Del, told her. Del was worried because Carl wasn't just doing cocaine; he was now buying and selling it. Carl was bothered that Mom knew because she made it out to be worse than it really was and he felt her disapproval. Mom sent him to get help. He went to see this guy twice and then stopped. Carl told me that Mom was the only one who stereotyped him for using cocaine. "She assumed I was on the way to killing myself and that I was strung out everyday, because this is all she knows from what she's read." Carl coped with this negative stereotype by explaining to her that he didn't use coke that often and that he wasn't to the point where he needed it. He just enjoyed doing it and nothing more. Carl has never been caught or arrested for having cocaine. He told me that he got rid of his scale so that he can't weigh it and sell it anymore, but he still uses it occasionally.

Perry was my brother's best friend. It was about two years ago at our house that Perry first tried cocaine. My brother was having a party and laid out some lines for himself and his other friends, Perry included. Perry never said a word. He just leaned over, picked up the straw and did the lines. He said he enjoyed the lift it gave him and the fact that nobody made a big deal about him trying it. He says he still does not buy it, but he does it whenever his friends offer it to him.

Billy, another of Carl's friends, first tried cocaine before he moved here. His girlfriend at the time had half a gram that one of her friends had given her for her birthday. Billy first tried it at her party. He said they celebrated her eighteenth birthday by going in the back room and doing lines of her birthday present. They both stayed up all night and kept rejuvenating their high with more lines. After that he started buying cocaine for himself and for her. He told me that when he moved here he had no problem finding someone who had cocaine to sell. He met my brother at a party where there were "massive quantities of cocaine." Billy said that he enjoyed using coke because it eases tension, helping to break the ice at parties: "It brings people closer together and gives a great high."

Both Billy and Perry said there were no negative social reactions to using cocaine: "If people at a party didn't want to do it they didn't do it and if they did want to they could." Neither of their parents knew that they used cocaine, although Billy said his mother knew that he got stoned. None of them has ever experienced official social reactions to their behavior because, as Billy reasoned: "It's not as though we lay lines out in the street or sell the stuff at the mall. It is done behind closed doors; not for the public eye to witness."

My own experience with cocaine began with my brother, Carl, when I was sixteen. He was two years older than me and we used to do just about everything together. When I was fourteen, he got me to try pot and we progressed from there. I tried cocaine one day in our house with him, simply because I wanted to try everything at least once, just to see what it was like. I was curious to see what everyone else saw in it. We did some together but I didn't actually enjoy it because it left a bad taste in my mouth after it drained down from my nose and it made my teeth numb. It was offered to me constantly so I had plenty of opportunity to satisfy my curiosity. I tried it again a few times after that with my boyfriend, my friends, and my brother again just to see if I was missing something. I still didn't enjoy it, so I don't do it anymore. But if I did enjoy it there would probably be nothing to keep me from doing it, except for the cost, because there really isn't any stigma attached to using cocaine, especially among those people who use it. In fact, within a social circle, it can be a sign of prestige.

Cocaine seems to be a social drug because it is often used at parties. Cocaine is the "in drug" which leads me to believe that the people who have it will be the "in people" at parties. It is a way to make friends and gain status within a social group, as well as simply feel like part of a group. Cocaine is very hard to deter for these reasons. People do not believe it kills in spite of the Len Bias tragedy; they deny that they are hooked on it or even that there is a possibility of them getting hooked on it. Something that gives such a high in-group status is not likely to be greatly affected by social interest groups or anti-drug lobbyists. Using cocaine may be like playing Russian roulette, but many people still believe the gun is only loaded with blanks.

Busted for Coke
by Kenny Morgan

I had planned to discuss the world of cocaine use and the sale of cocaine to others. However, during my time studying this behavior, two of the people I was friendly with were arrested and charged with distributing cocaine. This happened right before my eyes in my own home. I had only occasionally used the drug for recreational purposes and had never personally been involved in the sale of the drug. I had known these people since early in high school and I am very close to their families. Both were living with me at the time. They had bright futures. Now their futures are very uncertain. Bernie graduates from college this fall and the other, Billy, has just graduated. I am unsure what will happen to them and I am very scared and depressed for them. This experience has affected my life dramatically because I am so close to these people. At one point I had decided to drop out of school because I could not think of anything else. I stopped attending all my classes and started working full time to help them pay for lawyers. The whole semester was going down the drain. It would have been so very easy just to drop out of school.

Bernie has been involved in drugs for a while: "I can't be sure but I'd say since about the 9th grade. Me and my buddies would smoke pot after school but nothing major. I started getting into coke in my second year of college but I only used it occasionally." Bernie had only been selling cocaine for a few weeks before he was arrested: "Two fucking weeks. That's all I was doing it for and I still can't believe that I got arrested. I never sold any before then. I was only selling it so I could snort for free. Hell, the money I was making was going to somebody else anyway. I was a small-timer, not to mention inexperienced. When the police came knocking on the door I thought it was a fucking dream. I've only seen stuff like that on the TV. I was actually busted for selling coke. I'm scared man. Real scared. I've never been arrested before and right now I'm confused. I can't believe God would let something like this happen to me. The worst thing that can happen is going to jail. I just pray God doesn't let that happen. I can handle anything else but not jail. I'm real scared man. As far as I'm concerned my future is now down to whether or not I go to jail. Anything beyond that I don't even consider. I am very close to my mother, as you know, but no way have I told her about this. It would break her heart and that would be as bad as going to jail. If I could live the last three months of my life over I may still occasionally use cocaine but I'd never go back to selling it."

My other roommate, Billy, was 23 and had a degree in engineering. He was still living in the house with me while awaiting his court hearing. I knew him all through high school and he was never much into drugs. He described his reasons for getting into drugs as having to do with escaping from the university atmosphere: "Somehow I had ended up at university with a bunch of people I didn't really like. I was doing pretty well there but I just didn't like the people. I met some other guys who felt the same way and they turned me on to some dope. Then I did some coke one time and liked it enough to try it again. I probably only did it six times in the four years I was there. I knew I would be kicked out if I was found out but there was really no way that could happen if you played it smart. Besides, I did drugs very infrequently during that period. There was a kind of closed society; the people who did drugs knew the other people who did drugs and after that it was pretty much concealed. You know the kind of place the university is. The people there are totally against drugs. They would love to turn somebody in for drugs. That's why

I disliked them so much. It's not that they would turn you in but because the assholes would just love to turn somebody in. After I graduated I started doing drugs more often, probably because they were easier to get and easier to use. I met this guy who had a whole bunch of coke and he asked me if I wanted to sell some for him, not for me but for him. The only thing I was getting out of it was free coke. That's all I wanted, nothing else. I didn't even buy it and I got busted for selling it. What kind of shit is that? And I got caught because I fucked up. One morning this guy calls up and says he wants to buy some coke. One of my buddies knew him from work. He'd asked him earlier in the week if he did coke and told him he could get some. Anyway the guy comes over and buys half a gram. He even did a line with me. About four hours later the Narcotic Agents came knocking on my door with a search warrant and found a quarter of an ounce of coke in my room. I'd only been selling it for about two weeks when this happened. I had only sold a couple of grams of the stuff. They took all my money and all the coke. They even took money that had nothing to do with drugs. I have to pay the guy who gave me the stuff out of my own pocket which is pretty empty now. Shit I'm lucky even to have a lawyer."

It is still very hard for me to believe that these things have happened in the past three months. It makes me very depressed. I really do not know what these people are going through because it is not my life that is on the line. I don't believe they will get time because of prison overcrowding but I cannot be sure and that has put me under a lot of stress. The worst thing that could happen is that their parents find out. I pray that this does not happen.

Chapter 9
Coping with College Life

Going to college is a big event for most people. It is often both exciting and rewarding. But to some, college can be very demanding and create a lot of unwelcome stress. These next four accounts examine what some students do to relieve their stress and cope with college life. In the article by Donna Hart the daily stress of medical school is handled by taking drugs. So far the substance abuse that we have looked at has been undertaken largely for pleasurable and essentially positive rewards, whether these are of excitement, fun, money, status or prestige. Although some alcohol, marijuana and cocaine users mentioned that they drank, smoked or snorted as a release of tension, this was mentioned as one of a range of motives. In Donna's case, drugs provide a release, taken in order to be sufficiently loaded to carry on, to get through the day, and to regain control over lives that have been lost to the job.

In Donna's hospital the student doctors convince themselves that they are not addicted by restricting their use to non-prescription drugs and by convincing themselves that the pressures of the work justify doing something to survive. Negative stereotypes are combated by the claim that detractors are only justifying their own moral standards "by negating our positive accomplishments with their putdowns" (condemning the condemners). Donna also distances herself from the moral contamination of being associated with other drug addicts. She claims that drugs do not produce a detrimental effect on their own bodies or society (denial of injury). Therefore, the use of other drugs is taken as evidence of the insignificant nature of their deviance.

Mental illness is not something with which we imagine university students to be afflicted. It is not an unusual observation that everyone at college is strange in some way or other. Strange behavior is manufactured as well as masked, accommodated to rather than labelled. Students gain status from being odd, standing out from the crowd for some peculiar fetish, or from just acting crazy. Some, however, bring with them deep psychological pain from their personal biographies, such as relationships with alcoholic parents, violence or sexual abuse that has never been confronted, a need to be loved that has never been quenched. Some of this results in "letters" to faculty to whom they may attach in what seems like a crush. Others may be obsessive in their need for attention, a desperate need to know that they make a difference, disrupting class to get it, or hanging out in the corridors with inane questions simply designed to beg time. Yet others may suffer their pain in silence, taking every piece of attention as a hostile act pointing to their abnormality or inadequacy and sliding slowly into seclusion and isolation. In the university environment this will be more likely ignored than draw attention to behavior about which something needs to be done. Whether these activities are justifiably defined as mental illness is less important here than the fact that they can be considered deviant. In the paper by Karen Peters we see the extent to which distorted perceptions of rational behavior can continue unnoticed for years. As Karen and her friends demonstrate, slashing the body as a release of mental tension seems perfectly logical to a tormented mind as well as being harmless to those socialized into self-sacrifice. The motive for Karen and her fellow self-mutilators was to perceive the flow of blood from cuts to the body as strength to escape from the pain of pent-up frustration and emotions in the mind. The reward was a relief of anxiety and the ability to cope with the pain and depression caused by others. The behavior is rationalized on the grounds that it is actually therapeutic and serves to prevent more serious action such as suicide, that it hurts no one except themselves. Stigma is dealt with essentially by secrecy and forming groups with others who also self-mutilate.

In the article by John Robinson about campus violence and vandalism by The Palace Boys, we explore the less obvious forms of coping with college life. We see that beneath the news headlines of a violent crime wave sweeping campuses there is a diversity of subterranean violent and potentially violent forms of deviance involving university students. Here the focus is on violence against others. We obtain insight about the meaning of breaking rules that limit the use of instruments of violence. John shows how violence can be a part of individuals' identities which in turn are bound up with their group identity. This process reflects an attempt to gain status by being different and by reasserting their "back-home identities." John has his own identity in the college atmosphere other than the traditional identities such as frat boy, nerd, athlete, etc. Through a denial of seriousness, John's fellow Palace Boys were able to counter the view that their behavior was a disruptive problem. They held the belief that if others were not so afraid they would do the same things. This was said to be demonstrated by the evidence of collective support for rowdy behavior in some public settings and sporting events. They also point to the acceptability and normality of what they do back in their home state, thus illustrating the appeal to higher loyalties and suggesting that they are victims of their present local, temporary environment. John's friends also believe that their actions are misperceived by others. In particular they are not understood by those outside the student sub-culture, from whom they receive the most condemnation. Since these people do not understand they are denied any right to complain and hence we find a case of denial of the victim.

The Palace Boys that John describes impose their physical violence on others and their property. They do this in part because of the satisfaction of demonstrating group power. There are clearly objections from others to the use of violence and there is no way that this form of deviance can be considered a victimless crime. The principal objection is the danger to others' person or property. In spite of these complaints, however, participants still find little difficulty in excusing or justifying their behavior to others.

Given the ease with which justifications can be found for flaunting rules against violence or potential violence, it is difficult to see how stigma and social control can attach to this activity. However, it also seems that the most potent consideration is the generalized disapproval by the other members of the deviant subculture, involving, as it does, derogatory labelling combined with the knowledge that friends or family might find out.

When Louis Moss and his friends are terrorizing fellow students by firing bottle rockets from an improvised mortar set up at their college dorm window, they describe an intense excitement that can't occur in the classroom from a lecture. Part of the thrill comes from a motive which is shared by others engaged in deviance; the danger and challenge from breaking rules and getting away with it. The excitement itself serves to alleviate the boredom of daily college existence. Part of the fun and excitement, as Louis shows, comes from the related satisfaction of students "creating their own entertainment . . . because legal entertainment is not appealing."

These four accounts reveal the now familiar array of neutralization techniques, ranging from those friends of John who believed they had the right to do what they decided was important rather than what others wanted; Donna's fellow medical students taking drugs to relieve the stress of school, no matter what anyone else thought; and in Karen's account, the claim of individuality, in which she doesn't care what anyone else thinks.

Another motive that seems common to these accounts, but is less evident in other forms of deviance, is that of power and its association with perceptions of manliness. Louis talks of the feeling of power that comes from owning weapons and being able to command destruction. There is, he says, "a natural high that comes from watching something deteriorate as a result of your own actions."

The denial of seriousness was supplemented by another version of the idea that deviance is functional. For example, in the case of the communist assault rifle, Louis's friends operated the principle of "the better of two evils" in which they believed they were actually preventing more serious offenses from occurring should the weapon fall into criminal hands.

Every student has a way of dealing with stress. Some see a movie. Others talk to a friend. But in these accounts, copying with college life can result in disruptive and socially disapproved behavior.

Medical Students on Drugs
by Donna Hart

In order not to flunk out, medical students have to live, eat and breathe medicine 24 hours a day. Life has to be put on a back burner until after they have completed residency. Isolation from non-medics, anger and the close experiences with death take a stressful toll. As Bob explains, "I was putting in 36 hours at a time and it was just all getting to me. The attending gets on your ass. There's nobody that you can unload on. Somebody asks you how your day went. I mean, what are you going to say? 'Well, we got this 12-year-old who shot himself and while we're doing CPR, we're pulling out pieces of his liver on the way to the OR.' And they say, 'Oh', and change the subject. Pretty soon they stop asking."

A patient's death can be managed but it has a major impact as Frank illustrates: "I just drove around for a while trying to shake it. I felt embarrassed that I was still thinking about it. Everybody else finished up and went on to the next patient. It made me wonder what was wrong with me that I couldn't. I started wondering if I was cut out for this. But I had so much invested. Not just mentally, but financially. I was in debt up to my ears."

There is no release from the constant bombardment of the work, no one on whom to unload it. Some want to talk but don't know how. Learning the emotional maturity to cope with this kind of stress is not part of the medical student's education. Students come up with different ways out. Drugs provide one form of release. As Frank explains, "It was never a conscious thing on my part. I never said, 'OK, enough, I'm going to get snowed.' It was gradual. See there's no recourse to follow. You can't confront the attending. If you do they think you're not a team player. That's what it's all about—being a team player. Talk back and you're out of the program. So you learn to swallow your anger. When I'm loaded it doesn't bother me. But when I'm not I look for someone to dump on. Usually that's a patient. The attending lets you have it and you nod and then go off and see a patient and let them have it."

The use of drugs provides a way of getting through the day. It also allows one to cover up and appear to be normal. As Bob said, "I felt like I was going to explode, like I was going to go in one day and lose it. I started taking Xanax, at first just to calm down, just to go out there and face it. I mean I knew I couldn't walk around like that any more. I was afraid everybody would notice and think I couldn't take it. I started off with just .25 BID, just enough to robotize myself. And it helped. I felt numb."

Drugs are preferable over alcohol because it is necessary to conceal the fact of their use while on the job. As Frank pointed out, "If you drink, people can smell it. But if you're loaded they can't tell. You can explain the dilated pupils, the staggering by saying you haven't slept or you've got the flu." Being under the influence while on duty is facilitated by "bringing in something to smoke or snort" during a slack period and this will carry you through the rough. For Jim the use of drugs was an attempt to regain control over his life: "I wanted to desensitize myself. I thought if I could bring things under control, I'd be better for it. I'd be a better doctor if I could just control things." It is easier to justify if the drugs are from outside. Jim felt more comfortable using non-prescription drugs. "If you use real medication, then you've got a problem. If you use street stuff then you're not really an addict. It's not a real problem for me. It hasn't caused me to fuck up yet." This kind of rationalization was also expressed by Bob, who said that the choice of recreational drugs or street drugs allowed him to avoid confronting the issue: "That way I thought it wouldn't count."

Self-Mutilation
by Karen Peters

Jenny was upset and angry. She felt like hurting herself. "It didn't hurt anyone close to me, or so I thought. My masochistic tendencies became a release. At first it was a reflection of the pain, but as time went on it was a release from internal pain. It isn't easy to understand or pleasant to most people. It is a way out. I don't really enjoy it but I needed it as a tension releaser. The pain put me in a trance. It was all I thought about. I watched the sharp edge separate my skin. It hurt so much that I could hardly stand it, but I didn't stop. The slashes went deeper. The blood poured from my arm and with it the tension flowed away. I don't even remember why I did it at the time. It must have been one of those days when nothing went right."

Cutting the body with a blade releases tension. The blade, reflecting what could be power, symbolizes our strength to escape from the frustration of waiting with pain in the mind. Pain from physical cuts is different from the internal ache of pain within the mind. It is peaceful and soothing.

Jenny had never known anyone else who had engaged in self-mutilation until her friends discovered her secret. Brenda and I were also self-mutilating. Brenda got a great relief from her emotions. She said she enjoyed hurting herself because it made her feel better, seeing the blood. I think I did it partly because of Brenda but also because of my family problems. Self-mutilation became a release for me. It became a way to escape from frustration and psychological pain. If pain was in my mind, why not bring it out into the physical world where I could handle it? I enjoyed it because it showed me that if I was strong enough to cope with the physical pain, I could also deal with the emotional pain. Self-mutilation was a sign of my strength. I enjoyed the relief of anxiety and how it enabled me to cope with frustration, depression, and the pain that others caused me.

Jenny did not care what others thought of her outside her group of friends and most of them understood. They self-mutilated too. Societal disapproval was due to other people's inability to understand how, rather than hurting her, it restored her ability to think clearly and actually helped her. "They think it adds to the pain when it actually relieves it. Friends who don't understand often have problems being with me until my wounds have healed. They treat me like a child. They've often tried to get me professional help. I change the subject or ignore them. I don't like talking about getting help and they don't like talking about self-mutilation. So when I change the subject to masochism, they change it to something else."

Brenda said society completely misunderstands what we do. "They see it as an attempt at suicide and they don't see the benefits that I receive from it." She copes with this by hiding the behavior, explaining that it's actually helpful in preventing suicide. "I try not to take their lack of understanding personally. I do it for myself, not for anyone else. Once I started getting negative responses I simply stopped telling people and began hiding evidence of the cuts."

Jenny, Brenda and I were all very concerned that we not hurt others. We all believe it is better to hurt ourselves than to hurt another person. Perhaps we were taking on the role of those who caused us frustration and mutilating them. At the same time we never actually hurt anyone else. This seemed perfectly logical to us, given how we'd all been raised by our families to be self-sacrificial.

I continued to mutilate myself all through high school. Of the three of us, only Jenny continues to do it. Brenda stopped because it really upset someone she was dating. She said she might do it again if she felt the need, and it would not harm anyone other than herself. I realized that self-mutilation was no longer simply a personal issue when a good friend of mine told me I was hurting not only myself but also my friends and that I was also risking hurting my family. I began to see that self-mutilation was not taking other people's feelings into account. It was adding to the pain in my life. It became a turn-off.

Hooliganism and "The Palace Boys"
by John Robinson

I first met "The Palace Boys" about a year ago through my friend and roommate, Don. At that time eight of The Boys were living in a large dilapidated house across from campus which was named "The Palace." How it got that name is unclear but it is reputed to have stemmed from one of the past generation of wrestler "families" that had occupied the house. My first impression was that The Boys were just a wild bunch of guys from New York and Jersey who came to this school because of its climate and party atmosphere. I soon realized that the people I was meeting there, and in particular Tony, Skinny, and Steve, had similar characteristics to those of my old friends back home in New York. All were very sociable and all formed a very unified group with many similarities in their personal lives. Most in the group were currently wrestling for the school or had wrestled during their high school years.

The Palace Boys possessed a physical nature and personality which prompted frequent fights in The Palace, which were always in fun, as well as outside fights in bars and at parties against "assholes." These were people who did something to upset one of The Boys, such as spilling a drink on them or giving them an unexcused push. I have witnessed many of these fights since coming to know The Boys. In one fight in a campus club last semester, Don got into a quarrel with some asshole and ended up taking a cheap shot from him. Instead of taking on the individual himself Don pointed him out to the rest of the group. Every Boy that was in that bar swarmed on the asshole and proceeded to knock him senseless until bouncers broke it up and threw us out.

In other cases The Boys were instigators of fights. For example, we were in the same bar last semester when Don came up to Murdock and told him that some guy sitting at the table next to him had called him a scumbag. Murdock immediately got up and grabbed the guy by the throat and quickly the four tables emptied and a huge brawl ensued. One member's indignation is enough to weld The Boys into a group and this serves not only to let them display their physical prowess but also to show their group unity and loyalty to each other.

Besides having similar athletic backgrounds and being raised up north, each member enjoys drinking large amounts of alcohol. For one member, Steve, this was the major defining characteristic: "We're a bunch of rowdy drunks." Each person I spoke to agreed that alcohol intensified their own rowdy behavior. As Tony said, "It gets ugly after we've drunk a lot." The situations that arose would be much more violence-provoking after The Boys had been drinking. As a member of the group I often participated in one of The Boys' most frequent drinking activities, known as "Caps." This was a game with two teams trying to toss the most beer caps into cups. Each player was required to consume either six or twelve beers in a very short time, depending on the agreed upon amount. The winner was the team with the most caps in the cups by the end of the period during which the alcohol was consumed. A game of Caps was played prior to almost every time The Boys would go out at night.

Another aspect of The Boys' behavior included forms of spontaneous vandalism. The targets were almost always houses that The Boys were renting, including The Palace. Vandalism of this type was largely due to fighting after a Caps game. On one particular night, for example, the members of The Palace destroyed one of their houses and then walked up the street to tear up the other members' house. Sometimes their neighbors were included in these activities. On one occasion Tony, Murdock, and Skinny decided to construct a golf course out of the front yards of houses on the street. Tony was parring the course when someone threatened to call the police if they didn't stop.

Other acts against private property included their "work of art" on the back wall of a convenience store next door to The Palace. Over the course of three months the members had tossed anything at the wall that would explode and produce a mess. Items included bottles of ketchup, mustard, soy sauce, peanut butter, and anything else that would add to the collage of colors.

Each of The Boys developed their deviant lifestyle during their high school years. Their attitudes and ideas were already formed prior to becoming a member of The Palace Boys. Each member came to school and underwent a process of finding those similar to themselves to reassert their back-home identities and develop them. For some, this happened by chance at a bar or a party. For others, the introduction was through common friends.

The major difference between group members was the extent of their group involvement. A few of them had relationships with girlfriends which tended to restrict their activities in some ways. Others were less involved because of a strong commitment to schoolwork. Although these outside commitments tended to limit participation, they never seriously impinged on anyone's behavior.

The possibility of being reprimanded for their activities didn't seem to affect their behavior either. One member said that it didn't affect him at all, mainly because "there is always a way out," meaning that he could always talk his way out of it. One of The Boys mentioned a genuine concern for being caught because of his previous run-ins with the law, but for most the feeling was that they were unaffected.

The motives for the members' behavior seemed to be solidarity and the feeling of belonging to a unique group and the enjoyment of being different. As long as they received some fun and excitement for their behavior little else seemed to matter, especially what others thought. As Skinny said, "Doing what I want to do is what's important, not doing what others want me to do." Don explained, "Everyone on the campus enjoys cutting loose, but few have enough nerve or enough anti-authority attitude to just do it." It is because of this that many people actually like and approve of The Palace Boys. For example, during a recent university field hockey game I ran across the field in an attempt to score a goal after being offered $25 on a bet to do so. Although the officials were not pleased, the crowd went crazy with applause. In another instance of crowd approval, members of The Boys were diving into the crowd at a party with everyone cheering them on.

It is not always the case that The Boys receive approval, nor is everyone enamored by them. In fact some people feel intimidated by them. In one nearby bar, the owners were too scared to approach us after one of the members, Ward, was picked up and accidentally thrown through the ceiling. In other drinking establishments The Boys are allowed to carry on their antics due to their friendship with the bouncers. Those who get offended by the activities of The Boys, for the most part, seem to belong outside the student sub-culture. They include residents of the community, U.S. military personnel, and students having parties who are concerned with damage that might be done to their property.

Overall, the members of The Palace Boys perceive themselves as deviant and accept this label. They see their behavior as different from the norm but feel that many exaggerate their actions. For example, many times people may come by The Palace and see Red or Ward with a beer and automatically assume that they are drunk. In situations like this, where they are getting blamed for something that they didn't do, they express resentment towards outsiders. They also feel that they are victims of the environment since back home their behavior would not be seen as deviant because it is more common and more accepted in their home-towns. The Palace Boys believe that part of the problem stems from the in-state students who attempt to influence the rest of the community by resorting to "myth making" in an attempt to discredit them. In most cases this usually occurred by stereotyping The Boys as wild, uncontrollable Yankees that come from cities with low moral standards. This simply results in their further alienation from locals and a feeling of pride in their different beliefs. They will probably never come to accept the local norms as long as they attend school here, and will likely continue to insert their ways of life into the community.

Guns and Bottle Rockets
by Louis Moss

I was bored and tense from studying. It was 9.30 PM. I looked out the window of my bedroom and saw some students walking towards campus from the mid-rise dorm. An ideal entertainment opportunity to relieve my tension had presented itself. I had bottle rockets on my desk. All I needed was the mortar. I attracted the attention of my roommates and three other friends as I searched through the closet, pulling out the suction tube of my vacuum cleaner. They followed me back into the bedroom and watched in amazement as I started shoving ignited bottle rockets into the suction tube while carefully aiming it out of a partially open window. I hurriedly pulled down the shades and shouted out to them to turn off the lights. As students began scurrying for cover it was impossible for anyone to tell where the explosives were coming from. My friends were laughing hysterically, begging to take turns at the potential victims walking to and from the dormitory. As one of my friends, Steve, said: "The fact that these guys were clueless in trying to determine where the rockets were coming from made the whole thing intensely exciting." The situation had an element of danger but it was also comical. Fortunately, my third roommate was absent. He was a resident assistant and failed to find this kind of activity funny. After the supply of rockets was exhausted, the group dispersed and I returned to my studies. Such practices are an occasional relief from school.

On another occasion my roommate, Dave, came home boasting about this communist AK-47 automatic assault rifle that he had just illegally purchased from a street dealer. It came with 200 rounds of ammunition. He said that it was made in China. This added a special intrigue to it. According to my partner it is the best firearm that someone could own. Having something that not just anyone could get their hands on was a kind of status symbol. The feeling of possessing and controlling a firearm as powerful as an AK-47 also gave us a great feeling of power. We drove off campus to an isolated rural district to test out its effectiveness. There we set up several cans and bottles and began holing the targets. There was something deeply satisfying about this. It was very manly to possess a gun and to be jumping around blowing targets into small pieces. Dave said, "There was a natural high gotten from watching something deteriorate as a result of your actions."

Apart from the excitement and the sense of power that using these firearms and explosives gave, there was also a sense of originality and thought. My friends felt that by creating their own entertainment they could justify the illegality of the activity. Legal entertainment is not appealing. In fact, for us, it is not entertainment at all. Although launching illegal fireworks and possessing firearms was not the smartest of activities, since state and national laws prohibit the possession and use of any such weapons and devices, it was not as harmful as the law made it out to be. Besides, there was a certain challenge that came from not getting caught. Those involved did not feel that they were doing anything morally wrong. Those who heard of the AK-47 practice said it was "the better of two evils." This was because if Dave had not acquired the rifle it would have fallen into worse hands. Instead of target practice it could have been used to harm someone. So in a way we were preventing a potential crime. There was, however, some questioning of the ethics of Dave having an automatic weapon under his car seat.

After the bottle rocket incident we were confronted by some other students who'd learned of it. They were not part of our group. They berated us with the fact that this behavior was very immature and dangerous. We told the four who came to "fuck off!" One of our group involved in the exchange said: "If people want to disapprove of my behavior I don't care, unless they happen to be police. I feel that I shouldn't have to be confronted with their opinion. If they can't take a joke, then to hell with them." The impact of any stigma on us was not great since four people are not very effective at inflicting damaging stigma. As Dave said, "I don't think we've got too much to worry about. I think they feel we are a group of assholes, not a bunch of guys committing any major crime." We all took the view that those who didn't like the activity could think what they liked. It was not going to affect us or stop us from engaging in it.

Interestingly, although our group felt that being involved in an illegal activity without being caught was entertaining, they also believed that being caught by the authorities would be particularly horrifying. They pointed to friends and family members who would find out and that it may affect the chances of future employment. This was surprising because only one member had officially been punished for involvement with explosives and none of the rest of us had any problems with firearms and the law.

Chapter 10
Coping with Stigma

Deviant behavior, as we have seen, is not only different behavior but is negatively evaluated as bad behavior. Deviant behaviors may stem from physical or mental abnormalities and constitute what deviancy theorists call "ascribed deviance." Alternatively they may result from behavior chosen, at least in part, by the deviant actor, in which case they are called "achieved deviance." In either case, reappearance or repetition of the behavior results in eventual reaction from the audience who classifies these differences in appearance, function or behavior as negative attributes and labels their perpetrator accordingly. One of the implications of negatively evaluated behavior is that the person's identity becomes tainted, and this can result in what Erving Goffman called a stigma or "spoiled identity." This is likely when the behavior in question is magnified by audiences to the point that it is seen by both the audience and eventually the deviant actor as a major or master status, dominating all others that they might have. In this section, we see how stigma forms and how those subject to it try to cope and, in the process, distance themselves from the negative consequences of the deviant label.

In the first article by Staci Barker Wood, we can see how this stigmatizing process grows over time to the point of being internalized. However, Staci, a cystic fibrosis sufferer, ultimately resents and resists the negative labelling and marginalization and strives and succeeds at becoming exceptional at being "normal." Assisted by an eventual lung transplant, Staci transcends the stigma of her deviant behavior/ appearance and fully embraces the ideal that those not affected strive to achieve. Staci shows us how stigma is not only coped with through the management of information, but also how its effects can be overcome by the sheer will and determination to want to change the perceptions of the judging audience.

Debbie's article invites us to explain why deviant childhood behavior by her younger brother, Bud, has resulted in acceptance by Debbie's parents and other family members that he has a biologically determined mental illness. This is confirmed by everyone, supported by the fact that administered drugs have suppressed the disruptive behavior, that other members of the family had been similarly disruptive as children and is even acknowledged by the eight-year-old himself. A critical issue is the way in which a common definition is arrived at by the participants and how the version of reality that treats his behavior as mental illness allows medical social control to be imposed. In short, we see here an example of the social construction of deviance using the force of collective and scientific definitions. We also see how Bud's self-definition of this stereotype involves acceptance of the fact that he is sometimes not responsible for his own actions, but that with the help of the drug, he can become more responsible.

Nicole Senturelli provides another view of the role of stigma and self-labelling in her account of those who use the "alcoholic" label as a means of recovering from drinking through the Alcoholic's Anonymous 12-step program. She describes how members of AA form an emotional bond that is resistant to outside criticism and change and does not welcome those who refuse to fully follow the program. Nicole describes how AA members transform their lifestyles from active alcoholics to recovering alcoholics by sharing personal experiences with each other in the safety of the anonymous group. The extent of this change can involve replacing close friends and even family, whatever it takes to continue recovery.

Thus, whether ascribed deviance, as in the cases of Debbie and Staci, or achieved deviance, in the case of Nicole's AA members, we see how embracing the label of deviance can be one of the first steps to transcending it. Whether transcendence and recovery occurs alone, with medical help, or with the support of family and friends or even with support from deviant peers, these sections show that deviance and the stigma associated with it need not be a final state, but part of a process of becoming.

Stigma Management and Cystic Fibrosis
by Staci Barker Wood

When I was a young girl in elementary school I was allowed to leave the room ahead of all the other students who lined up to go to the cafeteria for lunch. I was allowed to leave five minutes early, go to the office and take five pills that were kept there. I would then meet the rest of my class as they approached the lunchroom. To my peers, I was lucky to be able to get out of class for whatever reason I had. To me, it was just something I had to do every day before I ate anything. I had cystic fibrosis, and had to take pills as enzyme supplements. The kids never knew, I never cared, and my disease went rather unnoticed. In fact, I was the first in my class to have a boyfriend. I won just about every event or race that I participated in at each Field Day, and I had more best friends than I could count on one hand.

In the sixth through eighth grades, a lot of changes took place between me and my peers. Throughout these middle school years it was obvious that adults had spread their "knowledge" about my condition and expressed to their children just how different I was from them. Admittedly, I was obviously different. I was far skinnier than any of the other girls. I coughed all year round—not just in the cold season, and I grew out of breath while running at PE or laughing too hard. My daily expedition down to the office to retrieve my pills was now seen as strange rather than "neat." I was hospitalized several times during these years, which brought awareness to me and my peers about the seriousness of this "difference" between us. Most still tried to be nice; some didn't, and wouldn't. I had friends, and continued to go to the "coolest" parties, but other than one best friend, no one attempted to come too close. The boys didn't look at me as they did other girls. At times I would hear hacking noises to mimic my deep, congested cough. During these years I realized, through the help of my peers, their parents, and my disease, that I was different. I realized that not every child got up two hours before school to have therapy performed on them and to do aerosol inhalers. I realized that not everyone took twenty pills a day and occasionally went into the hospital for weeks at a time. I realized that not everyone had another name like mine called something like cystic fibrosis.

I had been labelled as different, and had previously played into that role, believing that I had no choice. But I no longer liked that role and felt a duty to step out of it. It would be possible, but difficult, because I was aware of the uncertainty of my own future.

The summer before my freshman year I decided that I wanted to be "cool." I wanted to be popular, pretty, and have many, many friends. I knew that to achieve this I would have to change people's perspective of me. I got in shape and tried out for the high school cheerleading squad with my friend from middle school. It was tough, especially for me, but we made it. I continued to cheer all four years, winning awards and even becoming captain. I went to most of the dances our school held, as I also was involved in all five of the sororities with which the school was affiliated. I dated seriously, took trips with friends, and tried my hardest to be like everyone else, or better. I was still hospitalized numerous times and I continued to take pills every day, but my perception of myself threw a curve into everyone else's perception of me.

I often got tired of the acting, even though I told myself it was positive thinking rather than acting. Some people still looked at me strangely, asking questions such as, "Aren't you going to die before you turn eighteen? My mom told me you were." Most people though saw my desire to fit in and complied, perhaps out of respect for my attitude. I cheered, I partied, I dated, but I also took pills in secrecy, and coughed in the bathroom or behind muffled hands.

My label was wearing off. I was Staci and I did certain things because that's just who I was. A few years after high school I underwent a lung transplant to "cure" my CF. For the year prior to my surgery I was "Staci, the sick girl" with oxygen, a feeding tube and continuous IV antibiotics at home or in the hospital. Today I am "Staci, the girl with the transplant who is just doing so well." It's two different lives, two different perspectives, and two different reactions from those who knew me before and those who know me now. Sometimes I miss that other person. I kind of see her as my little sister, someone to look out for and protect. I'm always looking out for people like her. Sometimes it's hard to be different, and difficult to escape the labels that are so quickly placed upon you. Once seen as different, it seems that you are always different—if even just a little bit. People's reactions will label you as not normal, so how is it that you could ever be? To most in society, the likelihood that a deviant person will change, no matter what causes the difference, is unlikely and unexpected.

I wanted to share this story because I believe it illustrates how labelling attempts, and often succeeds, in personifying a person. At first, in elementary school, the kids didn't know I was sick; I didn't even know I was sick. In response, I was treated just the same as everyone. In middle school, my "difference" was given a name. I began to feel different as a result, as the kids often looked at me as awkward or intimidating. Once I made up my mind to change things, I began to look for ways to fit in. As I did this, others followed my lead. I no longer felt so different, and as a result, others no longer saw me quite as different. For the most part, I escaped their label, refused to accept their negative reactions, and went on to make a new person out of myself. I am still associated with that other (different) person I once was, but I have succeeded in putting it in the past. I am thankful for my "deviant" past, my "different" lifestyle. Without it, I wouldn't be able to see everyone as the same. I think this example of my life shows different aspects of the process of becoming deviant and recovering from it. My condition was ascribed to me; my recovery was achieved by me. Unlike most deviants I was able to significantly succeed in rejecting my labelled identity given by the social reactions to my disease. Thanks to a positive attitude and a transplant "cure," I was able to change my deviant identity. To some, though, I will always carry the label of a sick person, even though I no longer fit into that category.

My awareness of having cystic fibrosis cautioned me to the potential stigmas that would be attached to me once others found out. To me, as others have noted, the whole struggle was tiring. First, it was the initial acceptance (I was diagnosed at 6 years). Then it was the "selective concealment," deciding who was "worthy" to tell. I knew, especially while younger, that some kids would make fun, while others would accept me as one of them. It was often hard to decipher between the two. As it was to some of the subjects in the articles, talking about my illness to relatives, medical personnel, and friends gave me "therapeutic disclosure" by allowing me freedom to be myself, cough hard, or perhaps grow out of breath. I now realize that others were going through the same thing (my CF hospital friends). I also used "preventive disclosure" to "warn" teachers, very close friends, PE coaches and neighbors of my illness in case I needed to leave class to get water, wanted to have friends spend the night (early morning chest therapy!), or if I had to unexpectedly go to the hospital—the neighbors would know the reason. The last, most important "management of stigma" technique that I wish to relate is one that was quite valid in my life. The technique of "normalization" was used often, as I strived to be the best at everything I did, especially athletic activities. I relied on exercise to normalize myself with others my age. I waterskied, swam and cheered, all to my fullest capabilities. I thought that these activities would blend me in with everyone else. I was correct in this assumption. I found immense interest in these activities. For the discreditable person there are so many decisions to make about who to bring into your world of disease, while the whole time attempting to cope with the reality of a terminal illness.

Coping with Hyperactivity
by Debbie Bennett

My eight-year-old brother has been labelled hyperactive as a result of his past behavior and is currently taking the drug Ritalin to help him stay in control. This has caused our whole family to adjust our behavior to accommodate his special needs. Hyperactive children, whether diagnosed, taking medication, or not diagnosed, are stereotyped. Their excessive seemingly uncontrolled behavior is taken to be abnormal by their family and peers and is given as a reason for their need for medication.

Mom first noticed that Bud changed his behavior at the age of three when he went to nursery school. She had two other children who were 14 and 15 years older than Bud, and did not recall them having the excessive activity that Bud started to display: "We'd go into the grocery store and I was afraid to turn my back for a second. If I did, I was afraid he would start pulling everything off the shelves. It made me feel crazy." She talked to Bud's teachers for the next two years. They were very polite and said that Bud was "aggressive and very active but a very nice boy." Dad said that Bud responds to a lot of stimuli: "When we'd go to the movies he paid more attention to what was going on around him than to the action on the screen."

Bud does not fight with other boys. His aggression is limited to being bossy. Although he would make loud orders, he never resorted to physical violence. For example, on one occasion Bud was playing with one of his neighborhood friends. After playing with matchbox cars in the living room of our home, he suggested that they go outside and play, but his friend wanted to stay inside. Bud's aggressive response was, "I asked you over to play and I'm tired of playing inside. We're going to play outside." This led to an argument and eventually the other boy went home. There were many occasions like this one. One of Bud's classmates, who was playing at our home when Bud was extremely active, asked Mom, "Why was Bud born this way?" The perspective other children generally seem to have is that Bud has some kind of birth defect.

Mom asked the family pediatrician how she could better deal with Bud's excessive activity. At this time the doctor suggested that my parents be less permissive and follow through with punishments without giving more than one warning. Dad admitted that he, too, was very active as a child but had never been diagnosed as hyperactive. He has retained his active nature as an adult but suppressed his very active behavior as he got older, without the need for medication. Dad still experiences difficulties with some activities requiring discipline and concentration, such as spelling.

Bud's first grade teacher referred mom to a family therapist, Dr. Marsden, who specializes in hyperactive children and their families. Dr. Marsden talked with Bud and listened to and responded to his actions. He also talked separately with Mom and Dad in order to try and determine the cause of Bud's excessive behavior. He noticed that we older children acted as third and fourth parents to Bud which Dr. Marsden said confused him and heightened his excessive responses. It was suggested that my parents come to a consensus position on rules and punishments so that one of them did not negate the decision of the other. There was also an important symbolic reason for Bud attending the therapist with our parents. As Dad put it, "The importance of our attending Dr. Marsden's sessions is twofold. We want to know all that we can and we want to show Bud that Mom and Dad are both concerned."

One feature of Bud's behavior was brought out by the therapist: he became most aggressive when asked to do sequential tasks at the same time. For example, when mom would ask him to pick up his toys, take a bath, say goodnight, say his prayers, then go to bed, he would express frustration through yelling and throwing his toys. On other occasions he would totally ignore the requests, concentrating on the television or the game he was playing. The therapist advised our parents to give him no more than three tasks at a time. This seemed to have some positive effect and he became less frustrated at home. However, at school he continued to have difficulty with spelling, writing and reading. Mom said that the therapist had told her that Bud's learning disability is caused by "a lack of chemicals to the brain that helps him retain information and this same deficiency is associated with his hyperactivity."

In order to compensate, my parents made special teaching arrangements for Bud. Mom walked him to a reading tutor before school three mornings a week. He was enrolled at one private school and was tutored at another. He was tested for admission to an all boys private school but his scores showed that he was below the second grade level for English and at the third grade level for math. Such below-average scores are said to be characteristic of hyperactivity.

When Dr. Marsden prescribed Ritalin to Bud, "He became a new person," said Mom. "After several months of tutoring and taking Ritalin, Bud retook the admissions test. This time he scored at the fourth grade level in English and fifth grade level in math. Ritalin helped Bud's word retrieval and his retention of information. It also helped him to screen out other activity so as to increase his attention span."

Not everyone in the family approved of Bud being given medication. Bud's grandmother said, "I was very distressed. I had heard so many stories about overdosing." His uncle said his own son, our cousin, who is now eighteen, "was diagnosed as hyperactive but that he would never have him taking pills because of it."

Mom elected not to tell Bud's teacher that he was taking Ritalin. She followed Dr. Marsden's suggestion to wait several weeks and see if Bud's teacher had noticed any difference in Bud's behavior and his schoolwork. Bud's teacher said that nothing different was noticed, except that Bud appeared "more still."

Bud is very competitive. On one occasion, for instance, soon after beginning the drug treatment, he was in school and suddenly fell back into a bean bag chair. He immediately returned to his desk and his teacher noticed that his face was very red, as if he was embarrassed. Bud told Mom that he had suddenly felt strange and saw darkness. Mom, who was given quite a scare by this news, called the doctor and was told that the Ritalin might have caused some kind of reaction. As it turned out, Bud later told Mom that he had been competing with classmates to see who could hold his breath the longest! With Bud's competitive nature he held his breath until he momentarily blacked out. This is just one example of Bud's high motivation to succeed in competition with others whether in sports, school, or private personal accomplishments. Clearly, there is nothing about Bud that reflects a desire to underachieve.

In my opinion the use of Ritalin has made great differences. As his sister, and knowing him since birth, I recall several occasions when those with whom Bud interacts, including myself, had considered him a handful. I, as well as my brother, thought that he was spoiled: "He seemed to require a lot of attention and when he didn't get what he wanted he would throw a fit. It made baby-sitting for him very difficult. It was impossible to get him to bed on time. "

From Bud's point of view, he feels a certain sense of victimization. He told me, "Whenever Barry and you come home from college I feel pushed aside. Barry always bugs me and you don't let me watch my TV shows." To date, he has not attempted any verbal justifications of his behavior but he has denied that he was responsible for it. When asked why he yelled at Mom or Dad or why he ran away from Mom in the grocery store, he would answer, "I don't know why. I can't help it."

It seems to me that the calming effect of Ritalin has allowed Bud to better deal with these situations. In observing Bud recently I noticed a change in his behavior in situations which used to produce conflict and aggression. When confronted with play inside or outside, for example, Bud suggests that they play inside for half an hour and outside for half an hour. He says it's better to share and more fun too. I have also noticed a difference in his word choices. It seems that the Ritalin has aided in his word retrieval and he is utilizing a broader vocabulary. He has learned and now understands organization in writing and speech. In telling stories and jokes Bud is now able to begin at the beginning and tell the story or joke in a proper sequence. Although these tasks may be simple and natural tasks for most people, for hyperactive children it is a challenge. Hyperactive children find it difficult and quite frustrating to organize ideas and thoughts. Overcoming this difficulty is a real achievement for Bud.

It is difficult to determine whether Bud's progress is a result of the consultations and medication or if he is just becoming calmer with age. His grandmother pointed out that "He still has a lot of pizzazz but that could just be his personality and the average boy in him." There is no way of proving that Bud's calmer behavior is the result of medication or maturity. However, Mom testifies that when he is off his medication for periods he reverts to excessive behavior. And there is some sense that this is hereditary in our family. Our father is excessively active and his two cousins have been diagnosed as hyperactive with learning disabilities. These cousins were not prescribed medication, but each was held back in grade school. With Bud's family history it could be assumed that his hyperactive behavior is hereditary. It seems this is more likely in Bud's case than it being a behavioral disorder.

Although Bud's hyperactivity virtually goes unnoticed now, and his schoolwork has improved immensely, he will continue to be labelled as hyperactive. He will be labelled not least because our parents may fear their own labelling as inadequate parents. Because hyperactivity is considered a medical disorder our parents are not condemned but given sympathy. The label is comforting for us all.

Alcohol Recovery
by Nicole Senturelli

Alcoholics are people who drink excessively and who have been labelled by others as those who have no control over their drinking behavior. Some realize that the behaviors they are involved in are deviant and that they have a drinking problem, but may or may not desire to do something about it; others do not see anything wrong with their actions, and are in complete denial. Alcoholics Anonymous is a self-help group for recovering alcoholics who meet nationwide in small groups, large groups and groups open to the public. It was founded in 1936 by "Bill" Wilson, himself an alcoholic, who was also an adult child of an alcoholic. In order to learn more about AA, I attended several AA meetings and interviewed several members one-on-one.

AA members identify with each other because they have had the same experiences and have engaged in the same kinds of behavior. AA members distinguish between "active alcoholics," those who continue to drink heavily despite their continued loss of control, and "AA alcoholics" or "recovering alcoholics," those who have accepted that they have drinking problems and want to do something about it.

AA members have their own sets of rules, morals and expectations. They frown on outsiders, especially their presence during closed meetings of AA, believing that the only people who can begin to understand them are fellow alcoholics with whom they will discuss anything. Although they come from many different backgrounds, ages, classes and lifestyles, when they come together they see themselves as the same people with the same problems. Somewhat like a church, AA members will ostracize those who do not share their opinion, particularly those who refuse to go along with the AA wisdom or openly criticize its beliefs and practices. AA is also very resistant to change, but its effects are to bring a complete lifestyle change to its members, which includes changes in thinking, acting, where one can go and who one can see. It requires that an alcoholic take on a completely new identity. As a result it is often difficult for newcomers to adapt, and it often takes several attempts before they are able to commit to AA as an emotionally bonded member.

One of the main ways AA brings about this identity transformation is through the sharing of personal stories, especially with newcomers. Members listen to each others' stories and make connections to the commonalities between the speaker's story and their own, and from this deduce that they also might be an alcoholic. This approach is so strong that when I attended AA meetings I found myself saying, "Wow, I've done that," or "My friend does that all the time." It really makes a person think about the role alcohol plays in their life. If someone who is not an alcoholic can identify on some level with the speaker, it is very easy to understand the deep connection that members of AA have. They consider themselves family, each with a responsibility to protect each other, and the family as a whole.

Not only does telling personal stories help alcoholics who are still suffering, but it also helps alcoholics in their recovery. It helps them maintain their sobriety by reminding the members what they went through when drinking, and what will happen should they slip. One of the most common lines I heard at almost every meeting that I attended was, "You have to give it away to keep it." This refers to having to give your personal story to others in order to keep your sobriety. It helps "old-timers" maintain their sobriety and newcomers achieve it.

When examining the entire process of acquiring an AA identity and the programs and principles of AA itself, one can better understand some of the characteristics which outsiders view as extreme. Since members of AA have such a close bond, and since they discuss such personal and private issues, one can see how they justify frowning on outsiders, discourage skepticism and how they excuse their resistance to change. In order for members to acquire an AA identity, they need to feel comfortable telling their own story, and in order for that to occur they need to be able to identify with the rest of the members and feel that they are all on the same level. The more members have in common, the easier it is for new members to go through the transition of leading the life of a recovering alcoholic.

AA members are hesitant to share their stories in front of strangers. Some of the members at the meetings I attended told me that they are comfortable sharing their stories with each other because they know that they have all done the same sort of things, or worse. With me not being an alcoholic, some of the members felt I could not relate and should not be sitting in on a closed discussion. The members took a vote, and the overwhelming majority did not have a problem with me staying to learn more about AA. After staying throughout the entire meeting, and listening to everyone at my table explain how they first realized they were powerless over alcohol, I was able to talk with a few of the members. It was then that I realized the close bond that the members have with each other, and the feelings they share about members who do not conform to the way an AA meeting is run.

During an AA meeting, whenever a member speaks, they first state their name, and that they are alcoholic. At this particular meeting one woman introduced herself saying, "Hi, my name is Jane, and I am cross-addicted." After the meeting a few members came up to me to give me places and times of open AA meetings, and they began to talk to me, and to each other. These members were very bothered by the fact that the woman introduced herself as "cross-addicted". One of the male members commented: "Cross-addicted? What is she addicted to—crucifixes?" The other members laughed, and agreed. They said that if she wanted to talk about her addiction to drugs she should have attended the NA (Narcotics Anonymous) meeting across the hall. They explained that AA is a group of "recovering alcoholics" who share the same experiences, and that they cannot relate to someone who is "different," such as cross-addicted, nor can that person relate to them. The members I talked to had at least two years of sobriety, with one having over ten years. They were all very helpful, but they made sure that I knew I should not attend any more closed meetings, unless I thought I had a problem and was willing to quit drinking.

The second setting in which I observed members of AA was in an open speaker type of meeting. These meetings begin by two of the members reading the AA preamble and the Serenity prayer. The person who is then in charge of the meeting for that night, usually the secretary, asks if there are any newcomers to AA, and if there are, to introduce themselves. Then the secretary asks if there any AA members new to this particular location, and if there are, to introduce themselves. Next, the person in charge of the anniversaries goes up to the podium, and asks if there is anyone who has an anniversary on that day. If there is a person at the meeting who has an anniversary of their sobriety, they go up to the podium, pick up their chip (which acknowledges their sobriety), they get a couple hugs from other members, and they then go back to their seat. It is at this time that the secretary announces any upcoming events, and asks the other members if there are any other AA announcements. Then they take a short break, and wait for the scheduled speaker to begin.

At the first meeting I attended, I did not really want to talk to anyone, except for the man who greets people at the door. I just sat down, listened to the speaker, participated in saying the Lord's prayer at the end of the meeting, and went home. At the second meeting, a woman in her early thirties sat down next to me. During the break she told me she saw me at the meeting the week before, and she began to talk to me. I asked her how long she had been sober, and she told me almost a year, although she had been coming to AA for a few years now. She told me how hard it was for her to first come to AA, so much so she was drunk at her first meeting. She first attended AA because she got caught drinking and driving when she was a college student, and she was forced to go to AA by the courts. "Ann" and I then talked for a while after the meeting, and she told me why it was so hard for her at the beginning. All of Ann's best friends and her sorority sisters, with whom she spent most of her time, were big drinkers. When she first came to AA, the program was insistent that in order to succeed you have to stay away from people and places that serve alcohol. This was too hard to handle, since all the important people in Ann's life drank. She said that she slipped many times in the first couple years of attending AA, but then met a "sponsor," (a long-standing member who befriends a newcomer) named Jan with whom she easily identified. She told me, "Listening to Jan tell me her story sounded like she was telling mine." Ann said this really helped her to try and stay sober, and consequently she has been sober for almost a year. Ann barely sees her drinking friends now, but she hopes to someday get them involved in the program as well.

The third meeting I attended was with a panel of AA members who were all residents of a long-term residential treatment program. Some of them were still residing at the program, while others were living elsewhere and attending the program on an outpatient basis. This program incorporates many levels of therapy along with attending AA/NA meetings every day. All of the members with whom I spoke had relapsed several times after attending AA/NA meetings, and after having various other forms of treatment. What this program provides is structure and discipline, which requires that they attend AA/NA meetings along with therapy, and if members do not follow the strict regimen they will no longer be welcomed.

When talking with the members I found out they all agreed on one thing. Although the program requires a tremendous amount of work, the structure that it provides along with the structure of AA is what these people needed. Previously these members thought that AA was a good treatment program, but not for them. Although they attended meetings they never really "did the steps," nor did anything AA said was necessary for recovery. Many of them would go to meetings drunk or high just to fulfill their court obligation, or satisfy a loved one. AA will not work for someone who is not willing to conform to the AA way of life. Now by attending AA meetings every day, and by following the program's requirements, they believe AA has changed their lives.

One of the program's members named "Jack" told me his story. Jack suffered many periods of relapse during his long recovery. He is in his mid to late fifties, and first started attending AA in his early thirties. He was sober for over ten years until he was diagnosed with cancer and had to have surgery. It was then that he developed a severe addiction to prescription medication. He ended up attending a treatment program, and is now again attending AA. Jack has now been sober for almost two years. He believes the reason AA did not work for him in the beginning is because he tried to analyze everything. He wanted to know and understand why everything worked. Although other members told him not to try and figure out everything, just to let it work, that was not good enough for him. After awhile he stopped attending meetings altogether, because he thought he could handle his own recovery. Jack now admits that recovery is not something someone can do by himself, and this time he did his "90 meetings in 90 days," and still attends meetings several times a week. When asked if AA does not work for certain people, Jack answered, "There is nobody too dumb for AA, but there are a lot of people too smart for it."

So what is it that draws these people so closely together that their lives and identities are transformed? Is it the deviant behaviors they once engaged in, or the actions they participate in now? After studying these people I believe it is a little of both. The deviant behaviors they once engaged in, and the painful consequences they endured are what first allow them to identify with each other. It is what initially brings them together, and without these behaviors they would not be there. The actions they participate in through AA draw them even closer together. They go through the same rituals each time they meet, saying the same things, and acting in the same way. They share the most personal events in their lives, and do not pass any judgments about anyone else. They hug each other, hold each other's hands, laugh together, and cry together. They do not allow for "outsiders" or for those who will not conform to their shared values and beliefs. This makes for an even more closely bonded group, dependent on each other and on the program of Alcoholics Anonymous. The result is that people with drinking problems are able to replace their former drinking behaviors with the AA way of life.

Chapter 11
Alternative Lifestyles

The student accounts in this final chapter show us that deviant behaviors need not only be motivated by short-term satisfactions, nor need they only be justified by rationalizations immediately at hand. The contributors show us that the motives and rationale for deviant behavior may be part of a comprehensive belief system that forms a counter-cultural lifestyle. In many ways these accounts show us that deviance can be the outcome of a critical stance toward the rest of society and an attempt to construct alternatives within it. Indeed, it would be somewhat false to separate motives from justifications in these cases because the two are integrally related through their critical perspective on the conventional social order. For example, the central philosophy for the weapons offenses that Gary Fisher and his friends commit has to do with the need to survive a major breakdown in society's law and order. Like militia movements in general, their criticism is that society is too liberal and too prone to instability. Such a broad motivational context does not preclude deviant activities having ancillary motives, such as the illegal paramilitary training exercises being exhilarating fun. However, the meaning of any one piece of deviant action must be taken in the wider context of the philosophy of survivalism and militias, which itself is tied up with an ideology of individuality and patriarchy. Not surprisingly, when such people excuse or justify their behavior, they present their view of what is wrong with the society as well as what is right with their chosen behavior. Thus Gary talks of the need for self-defense in a hostile world, about those political threats to traditional values, and about how

153

survivalist members have been misrepresented by the media as vigilantes or worse.

Similarly, Susan King shows us that beneath the style and outrageousness of the "new wavers" there is a philosophy of anti-superficiality; a complex and critical set of beliefs that denies the straight world of materialism, consumerism and conformity, by ridiculing it and by expressing total disregard for such values. What might appear on the surface to be explained, for example, as adolescent rebellion to parents, is only a microcosm of these deviants' broader reaction to the society that their parents or "preppies" represent. Of course, hard core punk bands may provide an immediate escape from the constraints of a world that bears down on those who so blatantly oppose it, but escape is so inadequate an expression of the totality of meaning that shapes these people's deviant shock tactics. As Susan points out, the primary focus of the positive side of new waver philosophy is total individuality; the total acceptance of anyone who is different, whatever the grounds, and the total rejection of anyone who rejects or condemns others. It is interesting that new wavers adopt the color black in their dress since theirs is a truly anarchistic individualism that has no need to entertain excuse or justification. Instead they abuse that which constrains and oppresses, from whatever quarter it may come.

Tara Storm's account also describes a subculture whose main expression of difference appears through dress. In this case the art of "body piercing" is seen as a form of individual rebellion, specifically against parents and conventional society by some, and for others motives may be as simple as choice or sexual pleasure. She reveals that generation Xers, who have popularized this behavior, are, like the 1980s new wavers, expressing their difference and contempt for the normalcy and hypocrisy of the generation that preceded them. But she also points out that not everyone who adopts the fad of body piercing shares a common rebellious philosophy.

The critical thrust of the vegetarians discussed in the paper by Helen Marsh, and the naturists discussed by Jenny Cox, is directed at conventional eating and clothing behavior, respectively. Both papers represent different aspects of a celebration of humanism; the preservation of all animal life, and a concern not to mask the human form. But, as in the other contributions to this chapter, the wider philosophy which motivates and justifies these activities is concerned with contradictions and the hypocrisy of conventionality. That we eat animal meat but not people seems totally illogical to Helen's friends. She discusses the ways in which the conventional society tries to avoid dealing with these issues by their use of stereotyping and, in the process, how outsiders totally misrepresent their eating activity. In one of the most elaborated examples that we have seen so far of the justification "condemning the condemners," one of Helen's friends presents the typology of misrepresenters through which she condemns all outsiders, even those sympathetic, for being narrow-minded. As this deviant eater summarizes the position: "Vegetarianism is as much a position as it is a behavior. It reflects a moral stance."

The same condemnations are experienced by Jenny's friends who find that they are stimulated by not wearing clothes. The laws and restrictions placed on such naturists are condemned because they reflect confusion and fear rather than any rationality. What we glimpse here also is the politics of deviant groups. While it is true that the principal critique of naturist is against a clothed society which restricts the activities of those who want to go unclothed, it is also the case that considerable energy is spent protesting other groups such as nudists. The objection is that nudists are actually conceding the wider society's position by accepting that their behavior is something that should be contained in camps or colonies. For naturists no such apologia is necessary.

Survivalism
by Gary Fisher

In the nuclear age society is faced with the potential of the major destruction of organized government, anarchy and the destruction of the human race. Individuals' reactions to such scenarios include escapism, drug use, joining religious cults and immersing themselves in carnal pleasures, all an attempt to get away from the pressure of living in a world that may end at any moment. There are some, however, who believe that life is worth living no matter how bad it gets. Survivalists are the paramilitary groups that exist with the aim of ensuring their members' survival in the event of a major breakdown in law and order. They feel that life will not end after nuclear war or economic collapse for those who are prepared. They prepare themselves materially and in so doing keep their mind off the impending calamity.

Their behavior is largely normal. They work, eat, sleep, go to school, and have fun just like everyone else. Their philosophy is that survival should be an active offensive goal. One must not sit back and let oneself die. One must be able to protect life and property after the collapse of government. Thus they are very much concerned with current world political issues. Their principal clash with the current government stems from the breaking of weapons laws and regulations. Most members will not register their weapons with the proper authorities, and many will buy or manufacture fully automatic weapons without legal permit and undertake illegal paramilitary training. Beyond meetings, training, and subscribing to magazines like *Gung-Ho*, some will carry out active patrol duties outside of government controls and raise the specter of "vigilantes."

I am a member of one such survivalist group which includes college students, a police officer and grocery chain store manager. We do not have any stereotypical rednecks or religious fanatics who are often supposed to be associated with survivalist groups. Typically we meet a few times a month, mostly on weekends, at some remote rural site. There we gather to talk for awhile. On this particular occasion the conversation ranges from small talk to world politics and is particularly concerned with the status of world conflicts such as Afghanistan, El Salvador, Nicaragua and Lebanon. Talk also includes discussion of individual arms deals. It includes a "tip" on where to get illegal weapons and explosives. The conversation moves to helpful hints for the less experienced in the group.

The circle breaks momentarily for the members to secure their equipment. Plans for today include a mock attack on an abandoned farmhouse and barn. Our equipment includes automatic weapons, assault rifles, smoke and tear gas grenades, and explosives. This will be used to gain entrance to the "fortified" farmhouse. The members with a military background brief the others on sound tactics for the attack. Loading the weapons with live ammunition we prepare to move out. Along the way we engage in muffled discussion of the plan of attack as well as talking over tracking and navigational skills. The attack is quick and deadly. Man-shaped targets inside are riddled with holes. The windows and door are blown open and smoke billows from grenades, masking our actions from outside view. We take the barn similarly. Cheers of victory echo inside. The attacks are exhilarating. Adrenaline flows freely. We head back to the rendezvous point where we set up more targets and take turns at marksmanship practice. Meanwhile some of the group exchange weapons and teach each other how to use them. There is the usual battle talk and bragging.

Soon after this the members split and go home. I went with one member to see his "stash." He has amassed a good deal of ammunition, several different types of weapons, food for about one year, and batteries and other non-perishable supplies. He has accrued maps, formulas for common explosives and other literature thought to be helpful. He assured me that his stash was small compared to the others I had been in contact with.

The members of our group that I spoke with all began their involvement in a similarly progressive way. It started as children when our fathers and other male figures taught us to hunt and fish. We took the meat home to eat. It was a way of providing for the family and reassured the male figure that he could always feed his family, even if he lost his job. Paul said that his grandfather would always end his hunting trips by saying, "Your family will never starve as long as you can hunt and fish."

The process continued in later school years as one learned to "defend himself or the honor of his lady." We were socialized to believe in fighting for what we feel is right. As another member of the group, Herb, said, "All our heroes in the movies fought for protection of self and family, to survive."

Later, as independent individuals, we found that it was practical to buy more groceries than we needed in case the weather got bad or we didn't have time to run to the store. Like some people invest in diamonds or gold, we invested in items of a more practical, barter value.

All gave as their primary motive for survivalist activity the security of their family. It is essentially the security of the knowledge that one can survive that drives us to continue.

In addition to proving one's worth as a provider and defender, the paramilitary part of survivalism serves as a release of tension, an adventure, and a way to work out aggression. Paul enjoys the "adrenaline high" of the attacks and ambushes. Herb enjoys "blowing off steam by blowing something up." Bobby sees it as a "welcome bit of excitement." It seems that we all seek a semi-acceptable way of working off boredom and aggression. If it were totally legal it would not be exciting. Skirting the rules is fun.

All agreed that the general public reaction is not sympathetic. Bobby described it best. He said that when or if they find out he is a survivalist, "people pull back suddenly, as if I had the plague." We attribute this to the media giving us bad press and promoting the idea that we are a bunch of crazed killers waiting to take over. Paul and Herb said they didn't really care what the public thought, whereas Bobby and I tended to gravitate toward a more concerned and distressed view. Bobby would like to be accepted by society at large and not just his peer group.

So far the members of our survivalist group have avoided legal sanctions. Several, including myself, have been "questioned" by the police about illegal arms, but none of us have been charged or even arrested. This is partly because we engage in secrecy to prevent any legal ramifications.

Most agree that the official political and legal reaction is understandable. They also see it as reasonable to want to keep weapons and explosives out of the hands of extremist groups. As Paul said, they also feel that laws "don't apply to us, because we are not criminals, or murderers, or something like that." They feel that since they do not have political aims there is no reason why people should fear them. Paul said, "We don't want to take over the world. We just want to survive." Herb reiterated the point by asking, "We don't want to hurt anybody so why do they fear us so?" Bobby was more openly hostile, asking "Why aren't the authorities out chasing the Mafia, or dope smugglers instead of pestering us?"

Maybe jealousy rather than fear motivates those who oppose survivalists. They have been successful in poisoning public opinion towards us but they have failed to show that the values of personal freedom and the safeguards of those freedoms that are outlined in the Constitution are not supported by what we do. Sometime in the future, should the true magnitude of the survivalist movement in this country be uncovered, the sheer volume of those presented as "gun-toting war mongers" may be so threatening that survivalists may be effectively banned. That will be a sad day indeed.

New Wave Culture
by Susan King

At the risk of being called a "preppie," a "wanna-be," and "Muffy," I, as a straight sorority girl, hung out at a university town bar known to be frequented by "new wavers." A "wanna-be" is a person who comes into the new wave bar trying to look new wave as if it were Halloween, perhaps dressed in a miniskirt and red Reebok high tops or a leopard minidress. Scouring your wardrobe so you'll fit in makes you a wanna-be. As a very closely involved waver told me, "No, Sue, you do not look like a wanna-be because we know you don't wanna be!" After initially being called "Barbie" and "Ally Sheedy" by some hard core wavers, I was totally accepted and eventually found myself laughing with people I came to really like and fighting with people I had been friends with for years. I was interested in finding out what it was that could possibly make people so unacceptable to each other. Why did some of my friends dress in new wave black and why wouldn't my other friends be seen in public with them?

Carol is a very close friend of mine who is also a new waver. She began her lifestyle just as something to do. But as she came to see how much it aggravated her parents she became more involved. Her parents have always been very strict with her, not trusting her with anything. At 21 she can't go out on school nights and has to be home by 2 AM on weekends. To "reassure" her parents that their strictness is not terribly effective, she goes on shocking and upsetting them. She dresses in black whenever she can, shaving the lower inch of hair off the back of her head and wearing a pony tail that sticks straight back. Although hauntingly morbid by night, she is forced to clean up for college in the day because her parents, with whom she still lives, have strict rules: "My friends have to come over after dark because my mother is too embarrassed that the neighbors might see them and freak out." She tires of people asking her dumb questions about her appearance and her friends, and hates them pulling on her ponytail. She says, "Even though my house is big, when my mother starts yelling I have nowhere to hide so I go to my room, put my headphones on ten and blast hard core like Pistols or something. It's the ultimate escape from everything."

John had a pretty hard family life, losing his father and grandfather in an accident. He has since been challenging his mother, "because she nags me and I can't stand it." He dyes his hair from blonde to jet black and spikes it. We worked together all summer and he was always a popular topic for discussion on his day off. Our boss always questioned his position in life. "What on earth is wrong with him? He needs supervision."

The activities that new wavers engaged in were interesting. Late at night after the bar had closed about eight of them would get beers and go to some abandoned downtown apartments. The buildings were private and no one knew about their activities there. They would go through different rooms with spray paint of different colors. Many of them were artsy so it was not only destructive but also expressive. It was also exciting because of the ever-present threat of getting caught and arrested. This is a constant theme in new wave culture: putting one over on the boring conformists of society. After this they would go to an all-night cafe where often the waitress refused to serve them but they remained there for hours. Once they painted John's living room black. A bunch of them went over and made a party of it. John joked later, "I'm black. I am death."

My new wave friends and acquaintances walk together down the street, in a sense safeguarding each other from leers and comments of passers-by. Most of them are dressed in black with dyed jet-black hair or a bouffant, pale skin and black make-up, regardless of sex. They go to great lengths to pick and choose their clothes. They mousse and gel their hair until it stands straight on end and they stay out of the sun at all costs. They want to shock yet they want respect. Kelley was in McDonald's one night taking crap from a preppie university student. Her hair was a black straggled mop. She had shocking black eyeliner and ripped black tights with some sort of black mini T-shirt. The cross hanging from her ear didn't help. Her response was to scream at the top of her lungs. Everyone in the restaurant looked. Her friend grabbed a handful of French fries and threw them into the preppie's face. The scene resulted in a fistfight outside the restaurant which brought the police and ended in arrest. How can someone's dress and appearance lead to so much trouble?

The primary focus of new wavers is total individuality. They go out of their way to be nonconformist and don't deal much with monotonous yuppie, preppie types. As Kelley says, "I'm bored sick to think of going out with those guys (old high school friends) because they just go to pick up people. When we go out we go wild, have fun, like a family."

In contrast to conventional society, which is very intolerant of people who are different, new wavers are very accepting. As Kelley said, "When I go to a regular bar people stare at me and guys are rude. I get a hard time. But when these same people come to our bar we are totally accepting of them. We are open-minded and we don't care." Unlike deadheads, who retract from conformity, new wavers vent their anger into energy. Because new wavers accept people so easily it is not surprising that deviants in other areas tend to conform to new wave deviance. People who were unpopular in high school, who angered and rejected the popular crowd, are now headlong into the new wave scene. This acceptance tends to draw in a wide variety who are also sexually deviant and particularly those who are bisexual. Kelley agrees that it is largely because they are so accepting that bisexuals are an obvious group to find in new wave. It is obviously a reaction to society. They may be angered that their sexuality is not accepted, and react by being blatantly offensive and destructive.

Towards the end of the period I was confronted with having to make a clear choice as to whether to go out with my high school friends, who were conformists like myself, or whether to go out with my new wave friends. My high school friends seriously wondered about me when the doorman at the new wave bar no longer asked for my ID. One friend, Jessica, said, "As long as you don't start to fit in down there it's OK." And whenever I dressed in black it was a big deal.

Body Piercing
by Tara Storm

Nose rings, belly rings and tongue bars are becoming as popular as backpacks among the nation's college population, and among high school and even junior high school students. In some cases body piercers have joined together to form subgroups within society. In the case of generation Xers (aged 13-23), it is not so much the act of body piercing that is deviant, but the behavior of groups associated with excessive behavior. Their motives are formed by seeing themselves as outside the mainstream generational social system. What exists is a dividing line between a class of older citizens who find the physical appearance, behaviors and attitudes of Xers out of control. Xers themselves are striving for an identity and individuality through adopting strange or shocking appearance through excessive piercing of body parts. Excessive here refers to more than two earring holes per ear, piercing of the lips, tongue, nose, nipples or any other part of the body that protrudes. In some cases piercing has extended to branding, scarification and stretched earlobes, inspired in some cases by the pages of National Geographic. Xers believe that they need to find a way to be unique and individualized to show the world who they are and what they stand for. Their piercing is a statement to society that they are different, that they stand out and that expresses a contempt for normalcy, while they, at the same time, gain status and awe among their own generation. They are not just saying they are different but that they will live the way they want to, with or without the approval of their parents and their parents' society. As such they are a group of individuals bent on changing and controlling their own choices, without the constraints or oppression of what many Xers see as a generation of yuppies and hypocrites.

This ideology in non-conformity bonds the three distinct individuals whom I spoke to who had no other commonality. One of these is my friend Jane. At 15, she was not sure who she was or with whom she fit in. Jane says, "I didn't fit in with the athletic crowd because I wasn't good at any sports. The cool kids thought I was a dork, so I started to hang out with the alternative group. That's when I got my nose pierced." Jane is now a freshman in college and has a body piercing in just about every conceivable place imaginable. "They make me feel special, like someone stopping to admire a great piece of art, a Picasso maybe. It gives great self-worth and identity to realize that you are admirable, even if not completely acceptable." This statement by Jane explains how she deals with the criticisms of society and of the people who stop her on the streets just to ask why. Jane does not seem to mind the attention, questions and visual piercing from strangers. She believes that it is another way of educating others about her way of life.

Jane believes that the hardest thing about her first piercing was not the anticipated pain or the social stigma that followed, but the reaction from her somewhat conservative parents when she got home. Her parents were shocked over the newly acquired public degradation. Jane's parents insisted that she remove the nose piercing, but Jane refused. Jane looks back on the situation and recalls, "Things just got worse from there. They were always nagging me, telling me what to do. My father continuously put me down and my mother was always sad and hurt, like I had done something to her. They just couldn't respect my decisions. I was supposed to live in their shadows, in their world and I just couldn't do that. It wasn't my lifestyle. Anyhow, it made the next piercing a hell of a lot easier. There was nothing to worry about."

Still others like my friend, Chris, find different motives that lead them to piercing. Chris, a senior, says, "I got my piercing purely for the sexual stimulation associated with piercing, and I have to say it works." What Chris is talking about is that with a nipple piercing, the nipple will be more sensitive to touch and will maintain a constant erection. Chris also made a reference to the excitement when enduring pain during sexual play. This is accomplished by his girlfriend tugging or nibbling at the ring through his nipple. Chris's piercing is located on his right nipple and it cost him sixty dollars.

Chris believes that body piercing is not deviant, but he does admit that he got his nipple pierced because it can be easily covered and would not affect his employment opportunities. "I really don't have to deal with other peoples' ignorance of self-individualization. If I don't want people to see my piercing, they don't." Although Chris has a piercing himself, he believes he is different than the "freak" pierces by which others tend to label him: "I believe that piercing can get way out of control; if you have one or the other or one here or there, no big deal. If you have everything punched (pierced), it can get a little out of control." Chris believes that he got his piercing because he wanted to, not because he wanted to shun society, or to repulse anyone. He also thinks that body modification is a truly unique and personal experience and should be carefully thought through before piercing one's self.

Vinnie, a 26-year-old construction worker, got his first piercing when he was 15 years old. He accepted a dare from one of his high school football buddies. Though Vinnie does not feel that he follows the crowd, he says, "I was the leader of my crowd in high school. I was continually striving to be different than everyone else. They all seemed to take my lead and follow along." Since Vinnie's virgin piercing in high school he has gotten three other piercings. However, these piercings were all done on Vinnie's own volition, he assured me. As Vinnie predicted, soon after his piercing some of his friends followed suit and a new subcultural group was formed, calling themselves, "The Boys' Club Inc." Vinnie believes in his own self value and does not believe that he is deviant. He does admit that his group is somewhat different from the rest of society. He believes that people should do what is best for them and not worry about what others think is expected of them.

Each of my friends sees their situation in a distinct light. They are all aware of the prefabricated social biases against their choice of lifestyle. They do not wish to hurt or offend others, but only wish they were understood and accepted for who they are. They believe in themselves. Both Jane and Vinnie felt no reason to hide their visual modifications from the wider society. Chris maintained the option of secrecy. His motives had more to do with individual sexual pleasure, whereas Jane and Vinnie were expressing their identity and difference from mainstream society.

Vegetarianism
by Helen Marsh

At age 15 Linda had decided that she didn't want her life to be dependent upon any animal's death. She says that being a vegetarian means "not eating dead animals, whether cows, pigs, chickens, fish, or even cats and dogs—animals that I'm sure most people would find totally repulsive on a menu selection." As an owner of up to twelve cats at a time, Linda's refusal to separate animals into categories of those that can be eaten and those that cannot can be appreciated. Indeed, she goes as far as to say that eating meat is "cannibalism": "In the same way that most people might be said to enjoy not eating other people, I enjoy being able to nourish and sustain my own life by not killing animals."

Linda lived at college with my brother Mike and with Susie and there they, too, gradually became vegetarians by first going without beef and then going without chicken for increasing periods of time. All had considerable knowledge about animal processing in this country. Susie was particularly appalled at the way "cows are tied up, fed steroids and other chemicals to increase milk production and then sold to various manufacturers to be used as pet food, glue, cosmetics, etc., when they are no longer efficient milk producers." Susie's own goal was to "cause as little harm and preferably no harm, to animals as I can in my lifestyle habits." She believes that, "If you are able to eat a dead animal, you should be able to kill it, clean it and prepare it, then put it on your plate and eat it." She argues that most people would be appalled to do that but think nothing of going to the supermarket and picking up a "cellophane-wrapped piece of dead animal to cook for dinner." Her view is that, "If you can't go through the whole process, even in your own mind, then you shouldn't do it." It is, she says, "a contradiction of morals" to eat meat that came from an animal that someone else killed.

In addition to his respect for animal life, Mike pointed out the inefficiency of a food chain that involves animals eating large quantities of grain, between seven and ten pounds, in order to produce one pound of meat for human consumption. His argument is that if humans ate the plants directly there would be more food available and, additionally, grazing land could be turned to agricultural use.

Mike also placed most importance on the health considerations of eating meat. The history of heart disease on the maternal side of our family has given him added motivation "to eliminate the fat and sodium build-up associated with eating meat." He says that he actually feels better when he eats properly.

Much effort is required in cooking vegetarian foods in order to obtain complete balance of nutritional requirements. Where a non-vegetarian might serve one meat and two vegetables, Susie, who now lives alone, and Mike, who prepares all the meals for Linda and himself, will usually prepare five or six different items or combinations. A typical menu might include pasta, hot or cold; two or three vegetables, steamed or raw; some type of grain such as bulgur or whole grain bread; and fruits or nuts. The quantities are also much higher than non-vegetarians would consume. Preparation time is usually long since everything is prepared fresh with no prepackaged convenience foods used. In addition one needs a vivid imagination to come up with creative, non-repetitive combinations on a daily basis.

In terms of physical appearance and the effects of their vegetarian diet, it is clear that all three are thin but not in a sickly or displeasing manner. Mike has a very sinuous physique, much like a sleek panther. Linda has a figure that any model might envy, and Susie is also beautifully proportioned. Body fat is not in evidence. They do have lighter complexions than some people do but Linda and Susie are naturally fair, while Mike's profuse beard covers most of his once olive complexion.

Eating in public settings or with non-vegetarian friends does not seem to present any real problems. They all know which restaurants they feel comfortable in. Susie says that everyone else worries about her finding something acceptable on the menu more than she does. She says that she is perfectly content with a steak house so long as she can order salad. "In situations where finding special vegetarian food would be a burden on others, I am truly happy to go along, knowing that tomorrow or the next day I'll fix myself something extra special. I don't feel I sacrifice to be a vegetarian." For Susie, a dish of tomatoes or coleslaw will do if she can share the meal with friends. Mike and Linda, however, prefer eating at home unless the restaurant meets their vegetarian standards. A steak house is definitely not acceptable to them.

Mike says he has the most problems with people who don't know that he's vegetarian. "When people invite you over to their place for dinner, it's kind of awkward telling them that you don't eat meat." Part of the reason that these problems arise is because vegetarians are viewed as somewhat weird by the rest of the non-vegetarian population. Stereo-types exist that suggest "veggies" are just trying to get out of cooking, which we have seen is anything but the case, and that they look like "walking skeletons" with "pasty faces." The implications are of laziness and craziness. There is also a prevalent belief that veggies are stubborn and radical. For others, like our mom, problems are generated when she has to alter her behavior to accommodate the vegetarians. Mom feels inconvenienced by the whole process that she isn't used to and cannot understand. Her attitude has always been, "If I can't understand it, I'll criticize it." A similar attitude prevails among non-vegetarians generally, and can create considerable tension.

Mike says that most stereotypes describe vegetarians as "people who eat salad, have long hair and who live in communes; people who are trying to be in harmony with nature and who are very health conscious." He knows that his odd haircut, style of dressing and Abraham Lincoln beard cause people to think he's unusual, but he thinks of himself as being "a fairly normal person who believes it is wrong to eat animals." Susie says that a lot of people think that they are "hippie-types" or "religiously motivated-types," and she concedes that these stereotypes are accurate to a degree. She describes herself as fitting the hippie image with a "house in the country, dogs, cats, long hair and generally relaxed lifestyle." She finds people ask her a lot of questions about her eating habits based on preconceived notions and says that this gives her an opportunity to present an "alternative viewpoint."

Linda, in contrast, is less accepting of the stereotypical label and counters it by labelling those that stereotype vegetarians. "First there are the redneck/macho types who think we're silly, and that we only eat seeds, sprouts, and maybe quiche. Then there are health conscious people like joggers or doctors who think we're smart because we only eat healthy foods and never touch things like Coca-Cola, alcohol or Snickers bars. Third, there are yuppies who think that we are so good that we're the only ones still doing what everyone else was doing in the sixties and early seventies: recycling glass and paper, composting, gardening without chemicals." She cannot imagine how people can be so narrow-minded.

In spite of the existence of these stereotypes, no one in the group felt they experienced any stigma as a result of their eating habits, beyond the occasional awkwardness when people discover for the first time that you are a vegetarian. Mike said that most people are surprised to learn that his eating habits are simple and involve eating the same things that they eat except that they contain no meat, like meatless lasagna. A few others make jokes, but in a friendly way. Linda compares her moral convictions to someone else's religious beliefs. While she knows it may be hard for some people to understand her, she also resists the urge to "preach to them" about her feelings.

Although there do not seem to be organized interest groups against vegetarianism, it does require a strong commitment to different values to be able to sustain the behavior. Perhaps part of the reason why vegetarians are stereotyped as weird is because people generally are afraid to confront their own fears about cancer and heart disease. The fact that vegetarians openly recognize the risks of diet and attempt to do what they can to reduce them is threatening to the rest of us carnivores.

All rejected the suggestion that there might come a time when they will abandon their vegetarian diets. Linda said she couldn't imagine anything that could cause such a radical change in her thinking because "vegetarianism is as much a position as it is a behavior. It reflects a moral stance." Susie says, "There is no set of circumstances which would cause me to eat meat again. Even in the most extreme situation, stranded on a desert island with a cow and no vegetation, I could not see me killing the cow to stay alive." Mike says that he may eat meat in a life or death situation but it would be a difficult decision. At present he just goes without eating when he cannot be accommodated.

Regarding their baby, Linda said that she would feed her a vegetarian diet at least until she was old enough to "make an intelligent choice to live differently," at which time she would try to be as supportive as her own parents were. Mike agreed, but said that if their daughter should someday decide to eat meat, he hoped she would appreciate his request not to bring it into their home. He realizes that as a teenager she may feel a lot of peer pressure to behave like everyone else and eat hamburgers but says that he can only hope for the best. Susie says that if she has children and "if they feel good about killing animals, then I would not try to dissuade them or imply my lifestyle is superior to theirs. As I say people find their own way in this world and I would not think my kids would be an exception."

To these vegetarians the humanitarian issues are their primary concern. No one expressed the view that vegetarian foods taste better. But when I asked about "not eating meat" they would correct that to "not killing animals." Clearly, vegetarianism is more than a way of eating. Although still perceived as "strange" because of their lifestyle, they have become more acceptable in recent years due to the growing public awareness of the importance of healthy diets. As Mike said, "A lot of people know that it is a healthier way to eat but they're not willing or ready to make the extra effort to give up meat." For these three, the extra effort is as much a part of their lives as all those other attributes that make them human. Being human means being able to live in such a way that another life does not have to be taken to sustain their own.

Naturist Nudism
by Jenny Cox

The three men and two women who shared their experiences with me had all de-clothed before we began talking. Four of them had been nudists since they were children, and one for two years. They expressed a preference for being nude to being clothed. The newer member said he was motivated to participate by curiosity and by friends. They all shared the fun and enjoyment of being naked and the sensual, sexual and mental arousal that it brought. Participation in nude recreational activities enabled them to escape from the pressures of everyday lives, conventional living, business pressures or other nervous strains. An important reason for taking part was the sense of freedom as Bob explained: "I work a lot with rules and regulations. When I'm nude I can easily put all those restrictions behind me. I don't need anyone else around for me to enjoy being naked. It's a feeling that is unusual. It may not be a sexual feeling but it is something that you don't always have in your everyday lifestyle."

They considered themselves naturists rather than nudists. Naturists think they should be allowed to go nude in public places such as parks and beaches and they fight for that right. Nudists are people who will only de-clothe at a nudist camp. They would never come out from behind their fences to fight for their right to be nude because to do so would mean that they would have to publicly admit their nude activities. Jim doesn't like any categorization. He saw different types of nudists as different types of people who have taken off their clothes: "If someone is boring, it doesn't make any difference if they have their clothes on or not; they'll still be boring."

The issue of nudist camps was of central concern because these people believed that the public had misconceptions about nude recreational activities based on information from nudist camps rather than from naturists. These camps were seen as a "safe zone" for those who needed that protection in order to de-clothe. They also believed that most nudist camp members could not take their clothes off and feel comfortable outside of this safe zone because of the fear of being found out by their peers or the public. As Ken said, "They obviously don't get the same feelings from being naked as we do or else they would do it regardless of being caught." Bob felt that "nudist camp members are snooty intellectuals who have to have a purpose to take their clothes off. My wife and I have been to many nude parks, camps and beaches throughout the country. We have always been much more nervous going to nudist camps than we did going to a place where being nude is not legal. There is a feeling in these camps that it is not natural to be naked. Part of this comes from the camp rules that they impose on everyone."

Most of the group attributed the camp rules to the politicians that run them. Jeannette explained her experience of the camps: "We went to a camp where we were the first naturists to visit. The first thing we did was to introduce ourselves by telling everyone our first and last names. They jumped all over us because we gave out our last names. They told us that we should never tell anyone our last name at a nudist camp because we would be giving someone the opportunity to do terrible things with the information that could hurt our reputation. It was pretty obvious to us that they didn't believe that nudity is all right."

The group members were also concerned about rules that inhibited any form of body contact. They believe that these rules originate from the nudist camp members' fears of having sex related to nude activities. Jim explained that in his experience the camp members didn't even talk about sex: "I find them to be nauseatingly sterile."

The group felt that part of the uneasiness about being nude can be attributed to the puritanical roots of our society. Most Americans are confused when confronted with nudity so they deal with it in a strictly legalistic, moralistic way. Joni explained how this operates in describing the following incident: "I was on an unpopulated beach in North Carolina where women may go topless, legally. I took off my top and sat up. All of a sudden, a family with mom, dad, grandma, and the kids walked right past me and pretended not to notice me. The kids and dad slowly lagged behind, staring at me. The mom yelled at them saying, 'Don't look at that. You mustn't look at that.' They kept asking her why I had my top off, but neither mom nor dad could give an explanation."

This is also a good example of the problems that these participants have in coping with the general public's attitude toward nudity. They believe that because the general public is confused about nudity, they avoid it. In addition, because they do not understand nudity they react by establishing laws to ban and degrade the activities. Consequently, the problem for those who enjoy nude recreation is to understand why they must conform to laws created from someone else's confusions and fears about nudity. The participants explained that what is especially disturbing is that they can see no rational reason for these laws. They believe that sex is a natural human function and see no reason to impose rules on themselves to conform to other people's fears and misconceptions about what they do. They feel free to talk about sex, to have bodily contact with other nudists but not to engage in sexual activities with them. Because they are so opposed to conforming to the sexual rules imposed by the general public's confusion about sex, most naturists avoid nudist camps. Nudist camp members seemed to the naturists to be overly concerned with the general public's attitude that nudism is vulgar and indecent and, as a result, impose rules to regulate all nude activities. Instead of accepting the public definition, naturists choose to fight laws that are imposed by the general public that prohibit nudity in public.